**galloway
school**

April 1989

𝔇onated by

Mr. and Mrs.
Thomas Barrow, Jr.

ON THE
streets
The Lives of
Adolescent Prostitutes

Other Books by Elaine Landau

Child Abuse
  An American Epidemic

Different Drummer
  Homosexuality in America

Growing Old in America

Why Are They Starving Themselves?
  Understanding Anorexia Nervosa and Bulimia

ON THE
streets

The Lives of
Adolescent Prostitutes

ELAINE LANDAU

JULIAN MESSNER (M) NEW YORK
A DIVISION OF SIMON & SCHUSTER, INC.

JULIAN MESSNER and colophon are trademarks of Simon & Schuster, Inc.

10 9 8 7 6 5 4 3 2

Manufactured in the United States of America

Design by Joy Aquilino

Library of Congress Cataloging-in-Publication Data

Landau, Elaine.
On the streets.

Bibliography: p.
Includes index.
Summary: Composite profiles of young prostitutes, based on interviews, telling of how they fall into the life, their degradation, and the difficulty of making a change. Provides historical background and discusses available social services.
1. Prostitution, Juvenile—United States—Juvenile literature. 2. Prostitutes—Services for—United States—Juvenile literature. [1. Prostitution. 2. Prostitutes—Services for] I. Title.

HQ144.L35   1987   306.7′45   86-21825
ISBN 0-671-62135-1

For
Charlie Brennan

Contents

Introduction

ROSTITUTION AND SEXUAL EXPLOI-
tation of male and female juveniles has become an area of major attention in the past
several years. While statistics vary markedly, it
is generally agreed that major metropolitan areas
are experiencing a significant upsurge in the
numbers of female and male adolescents experi-
menting with and engaging in prostitution.

Juvenile prostitution is tragic. It frequently has
long-term psychological and sociological effects on
the youth and their families. Juvenile prostitution is mostly hidden. Recent studies suggest that
nearly 50 percent of youth engaged in the behavior of prostitution live at home.

Over the last ten years I have worked with adolescents involved in "the life"—prostitution.
Many of those youth are identical to those identified in this book. Elaine Landau's case studies
describe the two basic categories of at risk youth:
Youth struggling with issues of acceptance, sexual orientation, or sexual abuse; or youth who engage in prostitution through felt economic need.

Although there is overlap in areas of cause and effect, these groupings generally remain constant and have a direct influence on service intervention.

Elaine Landau has created a true to life picture of adolescents involved in juvenile prostitution. Her poignant and often graphic anecdotes compel the reader to want to understand the problem. Ms. Landau's skillful blend of factual information gives the reader the tools to do so.

Ms. Landau has given us a book from which we can all benefit. Adolescents will welcome her straight talk. Adults will be relieved by her sensitive yet factual discussion of sexual exploitation. Professionals working with this population will have a new reference guide.

> Patricia L. Dempsey
> Assistant Professor
> Hunter College
>   School of Social Work
> The City University of New York

The Hidden Crime

ADOLESCENT AND CHILD PROSTITU-tion exists in America. Owing to its illegal-ity, the hidden nature of the crime makes it impossible to know exactly how many young people have been victimized. However, it's been roughly estimated that between seventy-five thousand and one million minors in the United States run away from home each year and that over 85 percent of these young people eventually become involved in prostitution. In addition, thousands of other young people prostitute their bodies while still living in family situations of one type or another. While some young girls spend their afternoons having pizza with boys their own age, others engage in sexual activities with adult men for cash. In some cities, eleven-year-old boys frequent video game arcades, not so much to score on the game machines as to score with business-men who use their lunch hours to buy sex from a child.

Often runaway or throwaway children, these girls and boys are easy targets for exploitation.

With little education or marketable skills, no funds or family, they have to find a way to get by alone on the streets. After selling their bike, a leather jacket, or perhaps a gold chain, the only thing they may have left to sell is themselves. They use their bodies as a marketable commodity and soon become what is known as "sweet street meat." Some are as young as nine years old. This is their story.

Lynn—Age 13

It was freezing cold that Friday afternoon as I stood on the street corner looking for buyers. The harsh wind made the temperature feel as though it were below zero, and I had been outdoors for almost two and a half hours already. I was wearing a short fake fur jacket, a brown suede miniskirt and spike heels. Only a pair of very sheer hose covered my legs, and I shook as I smiled and tried to flag down passing cars with male drivers. The cold bit at my skin, but if I had come out dressed in jeans and leg warmers, I'd have never gotten anywhere. After all, I was selling myself, and the merchandise had to be displayed.

Finally, a middle-aged man in an expensive red sports car pulled up to the curb. He lowered the car window and beckoned me over to him with his finger. I braced myself to start my act. Trying as hard as I could to grin and liven up my walk, I went over to his car, rested my chest on the open window ledge and said, "Hi ya, Handsome." It didn't matter what they looked like. That's what I always said. I had learned early on what they wanted to hear. And it usually worked.

He answered, "Hello, Little Miss Moffet. How'd you like Handsome to warm you up on a cold day like this?" I wished that I could have told him that I wouldn't like it at all. That even the thought of it made me sick to my stomach. He had called me Little Miss Moffet—they always made some remark about my age because I'm so young. Being thirteen has been a strong selling point for me. In any case, I hid my feelings and tried to look enthusiastic. They all want a happy girl who they think wants them.

So with the broadest smile I could manage, I answered, "There's nothing I'd like better than to be with you, Sir." I started to get into his car, but he stopped me saying, "Not so fast, Honey, how much is this going to cost me?" I hesitated for a moment. I really wanted twenty dollars, but it had been a slow day and I had a strong feeling that this guy wasn't going to spring for it, so I replied, "Fifteen dollars and the price of the hotel room." He said, "That's a lot of money, but you're a real cutey. OK, then, get in."

We had sex in the same run-down dirty hotel that I always take my tricks to. It doesn't cost much, and usually that's all that really matters to them. Being with that guy was horrible, just like it always turns out to be. That old overweight man sweated all over me and made me call him Daddy the whole time. He really smelled bad too, once he got started. He may have thought that he was kissing me, but actually he just slobbered on my body. He kept calling me Marcy, and later he explained that Marcy was his youngest daughter.

Whenever I'm with a trick I try to turn off my mind. I just block out the whole experience. Sometimes I imagine that I'm on a trip to India or on safari in Africa. Anything just so long as I don't have to deal with the fact that this is really happening to me. You've got to do that to survive. It helps some, but it doesn't always work. You can never really escape from your own horror.

4

The guy kept talking about his daughter Marcy: how gorgeous she was, how fast she was growing up, and so on. He mentioned that on the weekend she'd be going to her first junior high school dance. His wife had spent far too much money on a beautiful new pink dress for Marcy to wear, but he really didn't care. After all, it was her first dance and Marcy was worth it.

Once he was finished with me, the guy seemed in a big hurry to leave. He dressed quickly, and just as he was about to rush out the door, I yelled out, "But what about my money?" He pulled a ten-dollar bill out of his back pocket and laid it on the dresser, saying only, "Sorry, kid, this is all I've got on me right now."

At that moment I wished that I could have killed him, but I knew that there was nothing I could do. I was certainly in no position to take him on. Ten dollars wouldn't pay for a place for me to sleep in that night. If things got really bad, I thought that I could stay with a girl I knew for a night or two. But that didn't change the fact that I needed money to survive. The middle-class man in the expensive red sports car had cheated his thirteen-year-old hooker. That meant that I had to go back out on the street and brave the cold again in order to find another taker.

And as I pushed my body off the bed, I thought about that man's daughter. Thinking about her made me wish that tonight I were going to a school dance in a beautiful new pink dress, instead of going back out on the street to sell myself to strangers.

Samantha—Age 16

I'll never forget the first time I saw Jerry. It was the day after my abortion. I was sitting at a drugstore counter sipping my hot chocolate and hoping that the warm liquid would ease the cramps that I was experiencing. The bus ride from Scranton, Pennsylvania, to New York City had been long, bumpy, and seemingly endless. When I got off the bus I'd felt sore all over, and that awful gnawing in the pit of my stomach was back again. It was starting to become a familiar feeling—the pain had come and gone at various times since the procedure the day before.

Maybe I was to blame for the discomfort I felt. The doctor at the clinic had told me to take it easy for a few days. He had warned against any type of overexertion. But under the circumstances, I couldn't help myself. My mother was so angry at me for becoming pregnant, to begin with, that she refused to speak to me as we drove back from the clinic. When we arrived home, I ran up the stairs to my room, packed my Mom's old brown leather suitcase, and sped out the door again. My Mom watched my exit, but she didn't say a word. I had had an abortion less than an hour before, but she still didn't try to stop me.

I ran to the highway. It wasn't very far, and I wanted to be sure that I left quickly in the event that my mother did try to intervene. But she never called out after me, and I don't think that she called the police because there weren't any cops in sight when I reached the highway, and that's the first place anybody would look.

A nice lady picked me up after about fifteen minutes and even drove me to the door of the bus terminal. She was really friendly. I told her that I was going to New York City to visit my aunt. She said that I looked very tired and pale, and suggested that when I arrived in New York I try to get some rest rather than tour the city.

Of course there was no aunt in New York City. I was beginning to think that there was no one for me anywhere. I wished that the friendly lady who had given me a lift could have been with me during the abortion. Anyone would have been better than my mother. My mother had been horrendous about my pregnancy. When I first told her, she had said that this was the last straw and that she simply couldn't handle me anymore. She felt that she had been cursed with me and didn't know why she couldn't have had a decent normal child. My mother added that she wished that I'd never been born. Hearing her talk like that made me feel the same way. Then neither of us would have had to face the other.

My boyfriend Tim had been even worse about the baby. We started having sex last year when I was fifteen. We'd been going together for a long time when I finally gave in to him. It was entirely his idea, but he won't admit that now.

Tim was the only guy that I had ever slept with. Belonging to him was all I had ever wanted; the other guys just didn't appeal to me. But when I told Tim that I was pregnant, he asked me who the father was. I had heard that guys usually ask that question under these circumstances. I think that you were supposed to expect it from them.

7

But I never expected it from Tim. And I didn't want to believe it.

Tim continued to voice his doubts about being the baby's father. I'm certain that he really knew the truth but just couldn't handle his share of the responsibility. Tim was content to let me face all the blame and humiliation alone.

I never found out if Tim felt guilty about his actions, because now he made a point of staying away from me. Even before I had the abortion I had heard that he was already seeing another girl and that he had told her that he and I had never had sex.

I didn't care. At least that's what I tried to keep telling myself. I don't know how I would have gotten through it otherwise. I decided to have an abortion, and then to get away. I felt really bad about losing my baby, but I knew that I couldn't care for a child alone, and it had become clear that no one around me was going to support my giving birth. I wanted to leave Scranton—and my mother and Tim, the people who had claimed to love me and yet treated me as though I were dirt.

New York City had always appealed to me. I had been there twice on trips with Mom and Dad before they divorced and Dad decided to just vanish from our lives. New York City was an exciting place. I loved Broadway and the theater district at night when the marquees were all lit up.

I had never been an outstanding student, but I had sung in the school's choir and glee club. Everyone always said that I had a good voice. I thought that maybe in New York City I could take a few acting lessons and do Broadway musicals. I hoped that if I could get a job waitressing, or doing something like that, I'd be able to support myself until I could break into show business. And if being an actress didn't work out, I thought that perhaps I could become a model. I had always been tall for my age, and I imagined that I'd probably just have to lose a few pounds to get started.

But as I sat at the drugstore counter in the bus terminal with my stomach twisting into knots, I realized that I really didn't know how to get started. I had taken two hundred dollars with me. That was all the money I had in the world. I just hoped that it would be enough to tide me over in a cheap hotel until I got a job. I told myself that I would get up, buy a newspaper, and find a place to stay as soon as the cramps subsided. But just then I wasn't quite ready to stand up, let alone pound the pavement for a hotel room. I really needed to sip the hot cocoa and relax for a few more minutes.

I noticed a handsome young man sitting across the counter from me. I realized that he had been watching me for about twenty minutes. I felt a little embarrassed yet kind of flattered.

As soon as I looked him squarely in the face, he approached me. I remember thinking how handsome and well dressed he was. Even now I remember that he was wearing this great beige suede coat. Looking at him made me feel awkward in my jeans and denim jacket. I hadn't packed much more, and right now I knew that I wouldn't have a great deal of money with which to buy new things.

The handsome stranger's name was Jerry, and

as we began to talk I couldn't help being impressed with him. Jerry was open and friendly, and in spite of the fact that he was a total stranger, I poured my heart out to him. I'm usually more reserved, but I guess that I just met Jerry when I was feeling vulnerable. Besides, his warmth and gentleness seemed to welcome openness. Jerry listened carefully to my every word. And at that moment, I felt both physically and emotionally drawn to him. I hadn't been so attracted to a guy since I had met my old boyfriend Tim.

Jerry seemed upset over the recent incidents in my life, and he wondered aloud how such terrible things could have happened to a young woman whom he found to be as sweet as she was beautiful. He said that it was fate that he had found me and that from now on things were going to be different.

And at first things were different. Jerry made it all happen that way. He wouldn't hear of my staying at a hotel. He said that it would be too expensive and that my funds would surely be exhausted in no time at all. Jerry told me that it's difficult to find apartments in New York City and that I was welcome to stay with him for as long as I wished. I could live in his apartment for free, with no strings attached.

Jerry promised to remain a gentleman the whole time and not touch me. He said that he didn't crave my body. What he felt for me was above that. It was all as simple as that. I was not to worry for any reason. He would hold my two hundred dollars for me for safekeeping.

I believed him, incredible as that may seem. But I hope that anyone who hears this story will try to understand what I was going through at the time. I was alone in a strange and very expensive city, and I felt that nobody back home cared whether I lived or died.

Jerry's apartment was beautiful—not in the way in which my mother would have decorated an apartment but in its own fashion. There were mirrors on lots of the walls, and the entire bedroom ceiling had been mirrored as well. Jerry had a round waterbed with a fake leopard skin bedspread on it. And there were furry throw rugs in black and red all over the place.

His place was much different from my parents' home or any of my friends' houses for that matter. It seemed wonderful. There was a sense of electricity and excitement in every room. Just being there made me feel like a movie star. As soon as I sat down on his plush pink velvet sofa, I started thinking about how terrific it would be to be his girl and live in a fabulous place like this.

At first I was a bit startled when after a few moments another girl came out of the kitchen. Her name was Terri, and Jerry quickly explained that although he had dated her some time ago, they were just friends now. He said that Terri had become like a sister to him and that because her own apartment was very small, with almost no closet space, he allowed Terri to keep some of her clothes there. Terri showed me her wardrobe. It was dazzling. There were beautiful beaded and sequinned gowns and dresses, a dyed black ostrich feather boa, and at least thirty pairs of high heels.

As she spoke I remember thinking how incredible young Terri looked and wondering if many young girls in New York City could afford to dress like that. But I didn't have time to ask her about it, because Jerry quickly took her into another room where he spoke to her quietly for several minutes. When she returned, Terri said that she wished she had more time to spend with me but she had to rush downtown for an appointment. She left in a hurry, and that was the last I saw of Terri for almost a week.

My next few days were like a wonderful dream. I couldn't believe my good fortune. Jerry and I spent every minute together, and he soon convinced me that he had fallen hopelessly in love with me. Jerry insisted on buying me presents. We purchased clothing and costume jewelry mostly. There were three especially beautiful dressy outfits and lots of silk and lace underwear. I was beginning to feel a little like Terri.

When I tried to tell him not to spend so much money on me, he wouldn't hear of it. Jerry told me that I was everything to him and that if it were necessary he'd spend his last dime on me.

Jerry sent me to an exclusive hair salon where they dyed my sandy colored hair blond. We bought a whole slew of different colored ribbons and combs to create various dressed-up effects. Nighttimes were wonderful. After dining out every evening, Jerry and I would make the rounds of his favorite bars and discos. He always introduced me to his friends as his "forever woman." And everyone said that I looked beautiful—something that I hadn't been used to hearing back home.

12

Within days I realized that I loved Jerry as well. No one had ever showered me with presents or seemed to understand me as he did. It was as though Jerry had stepped out of a dream. Pursuing an acting career meant nothing to me after being with him. Now I only wanted to become his wife. I hoped that we could marry and start a family right away. I hadn't given birth, but in a way I missed the baby I had lost, and I thought of this as my second chance. Only this time I'd be a respectable married woman.

I didn't sleep with Jerry for the first five days or so that we spent together. It wasn't that I didn't want to, but I had so recently undergone the abortion. Before I left the health care facility, the clinic nurse had instructed me not to have sex for a minimum of six weeks following the procedure. She said that after an abortion the patient becomes more prone to infection in that area. The nurse added that the medical complications resulting from such an infection might be severe.

I shared this information with Jerry, and at first we both agreed to hold off for a while. He said that he loved me too much to ever encourage me to do anything that might harm my health. But within days Jerry began to complain that he simply couldn't stand not being able to have me totally. He said that he needed to feel that I belonged to him in every way.

Jerry tried hard to persuade me. He stressed that now I looked perfectly healthy and that he knew for a fact that doctors always tend to exaggerate consequences. He said that once we made love, we'd be emotionally bonded for life. At the time I thought that meant that we'd be getting married soon.

By then Jerry had me in the palm of his hand. In my mind he had become both my life and my future. I didn't want to do anything to threaten our relationship in any way.

Physically, I had been feeling better lately. The cramps I'd experienced following the abortion had stopped after a few days of taking it easy. Since there were no longer any side effects, I tried to convince myself that perhaps the nurse was just being overly cautious in her warning to me. I had to hope that she was.

Jerry and I made love, and I was relieved to find that I didn't become ill afterward. I woke up the next morning feeling in perfect health and more in love than ever with Jerry. I remember feeling so lucky that I was okay after all.

Two days after we made love, it happened. Jerry came home in a foul mood, cursing out loud and saying that one of his business ventures had run aground and as a result he had suffered a severe financial loss. Jerry said that with all the money he had spent on me, he now had nothing left. Still, he stressed that it didn't matter as long as he had me. According to Jerry, I was still the only thing he really wanted or needed.

I felt responsible for what Jerry led me to believe had happened. I kept thinking that if I had firmly insisted that he not buy me this dress or that ring, then maybe he'd have some funds left over to see him through a financial crisis.

I asked Jerry what I could do to help. I suggested that maybe I could pursue my acting career as we had discussed when we first met. I thought that earning some money as an actress would help matters, even if I only got bit parts at first.

Jerry seemed to go for my idea but he reminded me that these things can take a while to get off the ground. In the meantime, he wanted me to have dinner with a friend of his who had connections in the theatrical world.

Jerry told me that this guy would pay to sleep with a pretty girl and that it would certainly be helpful if I got the money because he needed some cash right away. He said that it really wouldn't be like my having sex with another man because he'd know that I was doing it just for him. Jerry added that my going through with this would prove that I loved him as much as he loved me.

The whole idea disgusted me. I remember wondering if Jerry realized that he was actually asking me to prostitute myself. But I didn't express what I was feeling. I think that I was afraid to. All I knew was that the man who meant everything to me was in serious financial trouble and needed my help. Perhaps worst of all, at the time I believed that the extravagances Jerry had showered on me had probably contributed to his problems.

I decided to stand by Jerry and do whatever I could for him. I wanted to offer Jerry the support that my mother and Tim hadn't shown me. I wanted Jerry to be glad that he had chosen me.

My date or "john" (that's what prostitutes call their customers) was repulsive. He was fat and greasy and about thirty years older than me. To get the money I had to take off my clothes and parade around the room while he watched me and rubbed his private parts. I wanted to throw up or die or do something like that. As it turned out, we never went out to dinner, and he didn't know anybody in show business.

Still, I felt relieved when later that evening I was able to give Jerry the fifty dollars I had earned. Jerry held my head in his hands and covered my face with kisses. He said that he was proud of me and that I was the kind of woman a man could depend on. And somehow hearing those words helped to wash away a lot of pain I had felt that evening.

Although he seemed grateful, Jerry suggested that my fifty dollars was only a drop in the bucket. He said that we needed more money, a lot more money. Jerry said that he needed cash to set up a new business and that he also needed some new clothes so he could make the right contacts.

Seeing how well I had done that night, Jerry thought that if I could continue to have "dates" for just a little while longer, then in no time at all we'd be back on the right track. Jerry promised that once we became financially secure we could get married and that I could stay home and be a housewife. He promised that I'd have a maid and that we'd move to an even more luxurious apartment. Jerry knew how badly I wanted a baby since the abortion, and he added that we'd make one room a nursery and fill it with toys and stuffed animals.

I went along with his idea. I didn't want to disappoint Jerry at this point, and I hoped that my sacrifice would firmly secure our future together as a family. No matter how horrible it got, I was determined to get through it. I just kept telling myself that I was doing it for Jerry and our baby. Some of the guys I had to be with were really gross, but I thought that very soon my ordeal would be over.

However, during the next few weeks I began to feel physically ill. Jerry said that it was all in my mind and that I had to keep working, but I knew that I was really sick. I always seemed to feel exhausted lately. And now I found that I'd wake up in the middle of the night either with chills or with a fever.

I tried to ignore what I felt, but my condition only got worse. I had terrible cramps, and sometimes the pain became so severe that I was unable to stand. I felt about a million times worse than I had after the abortion. I was always feeling sick to my stomach, and it became hard for me to keep down solid foods. And as days passed, I realized that my glands were swollen.

Jerry was unsympathetic. He accused me of faking the pain so that I wouldn't have to work and do my share. He called me lazy, stupid, and ugly. Once when I said that I was too sick to go out, he slapped me so hard that I was knocked to the floor. Jerry didn't even try to help me up again. Instead, he spat on me as I lay there crying and said, "You get up and go out, and bring some money home, or you can sleep on the street tonight."

I felt terrified and sick to my stomach at the same time. I tried to tell myself that Jerry hadn't meant what he said. He had probably only spoken to me that way because he was under a great deal of financial pressure. Still, I couldn't deny that Jerry had dramatically changed over the past few weeks.

Now Jerry was usually in a foul mood and seemed to have little patience for me or anyone else. The slightest thing could set him off. I had also found out that he was seeing other women behind my back.

He was still having sex with Terri, the young girl whom I had met on my first night in the apartment. And she was also working as a prostitute and turning over her earnings to him. In return, he'd buy her clothes, set her up with johns, and tell her that she was his woman. When Terri first told me I didn't want to believe her, but when I confronted Jerry with the facts, he admitted it. I had suspected that something was wrong because Jerry had been away from the apartment so much, and it was becoming difficult to believe that he was out until the early morning hours working on business deals. Terri also told me that there were lots of other girls whom Jerry saw as well.

I was becoming more sophisticated about "the life" or the world of prostitution, and the painful truth was becoming clearer each day. Jerry was a pimp, and I was just another girl in his stable of women. Nothing more.

I didn't want to believe it or to think that I couldn't turn things around. At first I kept clinging to the hope that I could somehow rearrange our lives and make Jerry love me as he had in the beginning. But now that I was aware of what a polished con man Jerry was, I wondered whether he had ever loved me at all. Was it possible that he had just tricked me into entering the life to make money for him? And that he had never really wanted a wife and child of his own? I now realized that all the fancy clothes, jewelry, and lingerie he had purchased for me had simply served to make me a more salable item.

Yet I felt that I couldn't leave. For one thing, I still loved Jerry and hoped that somehow he still cared for me and that all this was just a bad dream. I also felt too sick to go. Sometimes I felt as though I were burning up with fever and that my abdominal muscles were about to burst. Once again, I found myself in no condition to go apartment hunting.

I was making quite a bit of money as a prostitute, but every dime went to Jerry. He set up all my dates, knew exactly what each one paid, and waited outside in his car to pick up the cash after each trick. When I asked Jerry if I could have the two hundred dollars back that he had agreed to hold for me, he denied ever having taken the money.

Once I put aside ten dollars to buy some aspirin and a hot water bottle for myself. Jerry realized that the money was gone and beat me with a coat hanger. The beating left my right shoulder discolored and sore. Jerry told me that in the future if I needed anything for myself to ask him and he would decide whether or not I got it. When I asked him if I could see a doctor, he said that we had no extra money and that I should stop babying myself that way.

However, a few days later, I did see a doctor. I

19

collapsed on the street while waiting for a john, and a passerby called an ambulance. I was taken to a hospital where I was later diagnosed as having Pelvic Inflammatory Disease. The doctors told me that the infection had developed because I had engaged in sexual intercourse too soon after the abortion. As I had ignored all the pain and early warning symptoms, my condition had progressed and was now quite serious. The doctors tried all sorts of treatments short of surgery, but nothing worked. The infection had spread and was too far gone. And the terrible pain continued.

Finally they operated. But the surgery was only a partial success. Even after I healed there was still a lot of discomfort.

Terri came to see me twice while I was in the hospital, but Jerry never showed up. When I called him he said that it was my fault I had gotten sick and that he was too busy to come to see me. He told me to give him a call when I was healed and could work again. I later found out that he had also forbidden Terri to continue visiting me.

What was I to do at that point? I had nowhere to go. A social worker at the hospital called my mother, explained the situation to her, and arranged for me to be sent home. My mother was surprisingly decent about everything, probably because they had told her how sick I had been. But as it turned out, my problems were still far from over.

After I arrived home, my condition worsened. The attacks became so acute that the doctors in Scranton decided to operate again. They told me that a hysterectomy was the only alternative left to relieve the chronic pain. At first I resisted and tried to live with the awful pain. I was only sixteen years old and still wanted to have kids some day.

But my Mom took me to see several doctors and they all confirmed that the damage had been so extensive that it was very doubtful that I'd ever be able to conceive again. I underwent the surgery, and eventually the physical pain did go away. But now I'm carrying around a different kind of pain inside of me, and sometimes it feels like I'm never going to stop hurting.

Whenever I think about Jerry or the time I spent in the life, I always cry. Not because I miss Jerry or ever want to see him again, but because I feel like such a fool for having given in to him that way. If I had had the sense or courage to get myself to a clinic or even to call my mother, I might have been able to get medical attention in time.

I had been able to go through with the abortion because I believed that I'd have a family when I was older. Now that dream is dead. And the only momento I have left from my loyalty to Jerry is my sterility.

The Pimp

A PIMP IS SOMEONE WHO LEADS women or girls into prostitution, secures clients for them, and then lives off their earnings. Although pimping is less common among men, some young male prostitutes have pimps as well. The relationship between the pimp and his prostitute is usually complex and may vary according to the pimp, the situation, and the woman involved. Commonly, the tactics employed by pimps in securing prostitutes include some degree of cunning, deception, or even physical force and violence.

One common ploy that is especially effective on naive young girls and frightened runaway teens is that of befriending the girl and later appearing to become emotionally involved with her. Easy targets for this con may be readily identified by an experienced pimp.

He'll be waiting at the bus and train terminals as well as in nearby coffee shops to search for young runaways who have just arrived in town. A young girl by herself who is crying, looks lost, or is struggling with her luggage is likely to attract his attention. The pimp is hoping to find a girl who is hurt and angry at her family, has little money, and few or no job skills. He needs a vulnerable young person, who on some level wishes to be cared for and will therefore be more open psychologically to his persuasion.

After initially approaching the girl, the pimp will usually do everything in his power to convince her of his warmth and generosity. He may buy a hungry girl a warm and filling meal and offer to help her to find a place to spend the night. His conversation will be filled with compliments for her and the suggestion that beauty such as hers should be enhanced by glamorous new clothes and accessories.

It may seem like a romantic fairy tale heading toward a happy ending. In reality, it's a common pimp ploy known as a love con. An effective pimp will play the scenario to exploit its full potential. He may not initially try to elicit sex from the girl. In many instances, these girls have fled sexually abusive home situations, and the pimp doesn't want to reinforce negative feelings that might distance the girl from him. He's more likely at first to try to gain her trust by making no demands whatsoever on her until he is certain that she's become infatuated with him.

After they've spent a short time together, the pimp will usually profess his love to the girl. He may tell her that she'll be his "star baby" or "foxy lady" and that he's never felt this way about any girl before. At this point, the pimp will be especially attuned to whatever it may take to win the girl over. Usually there will be opulent dinners, dressy outfits, lacy underwear, and if warranted, perhaps even an expensive fur.

The pimp may justify such extravagances claiming that he simply can't do enough for the girl. However, one of his primary objectives is eventually to make her feel guilty and indebted to him. And while the pimp may appear lavish in his spending, in reality, the girl's meals, shelter, and new clothing are tallied up to be used later as an account due record. The girl has no idea that she will eventually be expected to pay him back. And before she's even realized exactly what's happened to her, she may find herself financially as well as emotionally tied to this man.

It is essential to note that although the girl is led to believe that they are sharing love in a growing relationship, in actuality, the pimp retains his emotional aloofness. He is orchestrating an intimate power game. He cannot afford to become romantically involved, as he enterprisingly grooms his victim to enhance his livelihood. Affection and seemingly mutual sex are employed by the pimp only to further bond the young woman to him.

Once a sexual relationship between the girl and the pimp has been firmly established, and the girl has expressed her love for him, the stage has been set for the pimp to turn the tables. He is now in a position to make his own demands known.

At this point, in one way or another, the girl is placed in a position where she is asked to prove that she "really loves" him and is prepared to demonstrate her commitment to him through her actions. To show herself worthy of his love and affection, the girl must at all times be willing to do whatever the pimp asks. She is not permitted to set limits on his demands, even if they include selling her body for a few dollars.

If a girl refuses or even protests, the pimp will usually create a scene and accuse her of not caring enough about him. He may remind her of the money he spent on her, insinuating that he was there for her when she needed him. The implication is that she would not do the same for him, that she is ungrateful and undeserving. Anxious to restore the former romantic tone of their relationship, the young woman may go along with her pimp's demands. Although she may try to tell herself that she's only doing it this once, in actuality, she may be embarking on a viciously destructive cycle.

Once she gets through the first few times, the girl is usually firmly rooted in her pimp's scheme. Even after she has prostituted her body for a number of weeks, the pimp will continue to accuse the girl of being ungrateful and of not doing enough. Still attempting to recapture his once freely given love, which is now tightly withheld from her, the girl may continue to do his bidding. Her situation is hopeless because she is trying to regain what she never had to begin with. She is chasing only an illusion of love and commitment created by her pimp to initiate her into prostitution.

Even though it was the pimp who turned her into a prostitute, he will try to use what she has become as a weapon against her. If he finds that degrading the girl is helpful to him, the pimp will call her a whore or a slut. The pimp's rejection of the girl in the very role that he thrust on her, combined with society's condemnation of prostitution, usually serves to underscore the girl's own feelings of low self-esteem that might have contributed to her being a vulnerable target to begin with.

Within a short period of time, the pimp will usually require that the girl meet specific nightly quotas. He will take all the money she earns, doling out to her only what he feels she needs.

The love con has proven to be an effective pimp tactic on many young women and girls. Its success involves breaking down the girl's confidence and self-respect by alternating love and affection with rejection and humiliation. The girl is always made to feel that what is happening to her is her own fault. As a result, she continues to prostitute herself hoping to rectify the situation. However, in actuality, her pimp may have never felt anything but contempt for her.

Some pimps use direct physical violence in procuring and maintaining young women as prostitutes. This is what happened to a fourteen-year-old girl who ran away from her parents' suburban Long Island, New York, home after having had an argument with her father. Alone, confused, and frightened, the girl ended up somewhere near the Pennsylvania Railroad Station in the heart of New York City.

There she was approached and seemingly befriended by a pimp named Joey Ace who had introduced himself to the girl as Walter Johnson.

After talking with the girl, Johnson offered to act as an intermediary between the girl and her father in an effort to patch things up within her family. The girl felt that she could trust Johnson, and as she had no money of her own, she accepted his offer to spend the night at his hotel. It was agreed that in the morning the two would head back to Long Island together to speak with her father.

Unfortunately, that's not the way it turned out. Entering the Court Hotel with Joey Ace, the girl had no idea what was in store for her. Once inside his room, Ace demonstrated his complete power over her by raping the girl and terrorizing her with a long knife. He held the blade against the girl's throat and told her, "If you don't do as I say, I'm going to use this on you."

After three days of this type of continuous intimidation and abuse, Ace informed the girl that he was going to be her pimp and that she would work the street for him. He dropped her off in front of a large busy New York City hotel to scout for potential customers. But instead the girl ran into the hotel's lobby and hid inside the ladies' room.

When she finally worked up enough courage to come out, the girl approached one of the hotel security guards to ask for help. The police were promptly called, and the girl was returned to her parents' home. Eventually, Joey Ace was arrested.

Despite her harrowing experience, this Long Island runaway proved to be one of the lucky ones. Joey Ace's tactics had been calculated to break the girl's will and shatter her defenses. His mastery over her and terrifying manipulations were supposed to reinforce her feelings of helplessness and victimization. However, because of her own personal reservoir of inner strength and resourcefulness, this girl escaped before she was broken. Unfortunately, many others do not fare as well.

In the pimp's world, tactics such as those employed by Joey Ace are known as "seasoning." Seasoning is not an exact science by any means. Its basic objective is to destroy the victim's will and confidence. It also attempts to separate the girl from her former life. The pimp tries to take the girl over—mind, body, and soul. If he is successful, the young woman will almost literally become her pimp's personal property.

Specific seasoning tactics vary depending on the pimp as well as on his victim. Their form and extent is somewhat determined by the girl's resistance. In addition, the degree of sadism with which the pimp is comfortable also enters into this complex picture.

To strengthen the bond between himself and the girl, the pimp will generally do all he can to create a sense of dependency in her. Often pimps will take girls far from their homes to make it especially difficult for them to return to their families without money of their own or transportation. In instances where girls have been taken out of the country to participate in international prostitution rings, not knowing the language has presented a serious barrier to escaping from the situation. At times, girls may be given heavy daily dosages of habit-forming drugs either forcibly or otherwise. The pimp hopes that once a girl has turned into an addict, she'll be less likely to try to run away from her source.

Seasoning tactics are also used by pimps to keep women active in prostitution as well as to procure them in the first place. Young women may be led to experiment with prostitution for various reasons. Some succumb to please their pimps, some may be striking back at their families in anger, while others may just wish to experience the excitement of being a "bad girl." Often these girls believe that they can stop what they are doing whenever they wish. In many instances, they have no idea how difficult it can be to extricate themselves once they become entangled with a professional pimp who feels that he holds the deeds to their lives in his hands.

One fifteen-year-old girl who was procured in Minneapolis and later brought to New York City described what it was like for her to try to leave her pimp this way: "I never believed that Jake would ever really try to hurt me. He may have slapped me once or twice, or tried to scare me in other ways, but I somehow still thought that I was very special to him. I had witnessed his violent behavior toward others, but I never imagined that I'd have to deal with it.

"I was wrong. Really wrong about Jake. When I first told him that I was leaving him, he knocked me down on the floor and began kicking my face with his boot. I later learned that his little maneuver broke my nose in two places and caused a hairline fracture in my jaw.

"After Jake finished with me, he just left me

there on the floor. I guess he thought that I was too afraid to move or that I didn't have any strength left. But I did manage to get up and run out the door. I raced down the stairs hoping to get out of the building, but Jake came after me and caught me in the stairwell. Pinning me against the wall, he kept punching my stomach until I felt as though I couldn't stand up by myself any longer.

"Jake must have thought that he had finally finished off any hope I had of escaping, because he left me there sobbing and bleeding on the stairs and returned to our apartment. I'm sure that he expected me to come back upstairs to him as soon as I could pick myself up, but I didn't. Instead, I ran out into the street and stood in the middle of the road screaming for help.

"I was fortunate that Jake didn't have another chance to get at me. Some of the neighbors who had heard all the commotion had called the police. Within moments I saw the flashing lights of two arriving police cars, and I knew that Jake wouldn't be able to kill me that night. I was safe for now."

Young women with a small child have at times proven to be particularly vulnerable to being kept in tow by their pimps. Often pimps will offer to help the woman arrange for child care to enable her to work. However, the child care provided by the pimp is just another part of his strategy.

The pimp may offer to watch the child while the mother works or may provide transportation for the child to school or to a babysitter's home. In either instance, the pimp is afforded some opportunity throughout the day to exert physical control over the child's life. A prostitute who tries to leave her pimp may find that he will hold her child hostage until her return. If she calls his bluff, he may threaten to harm the child. In most instances, such tactics will usually force her back to work.

A crucial part of the pimp's seasoning that serves as a barrier to a young woman's escape is that of providing her with a new identity. The girl and her pimp will pick out a new name for her to work under—usually something glamorous or catchy. Some girls select the first name of their favorite movie star.

An experienced pimp will be able to provide a girl with a false birth certificate and driver's license under her new name. Even a new social security card may be secured. The most obvious reason for the change is to conceal the girl's actual age and identity if she should be picked up by the police. This protection may be especially important to the pimp if many of the girls with whom he is involved are minors.

What's more, taking on a new identity serves further to sever a young girl from her past. It enhances her loss of connection with her former lifestyle, her family, and her old friends. This division is extremely crucial to the pimp because in order to control the girl effectively he must erase her former set of values or sense of morality. The pimp's goal is to create an entirely new environment for the girl in which he becomes the center of her world. He will help her to put old remembrances and family obligations behind her. He will now choose her friends, run her schedule, and attempt to rule her life through psychological game playing.

In the pimp-prostitute relationship the pimp retains complete authority. He demands unquestioning and perfect obedience from the newly procured young woman. The implied message to the girl from her pimp is—"Just do exactly as I say, and I will take care of you." However, the role of protector is a façade that often tends to be in sharp contrast to the pimp's actual behavior throughout the relationship.

Although a pimp may claim to offer his prostitute protection from violent customers as well as from the authorities, this often proves not to be so. Many prostitutes have been forced to face sadistic customers alone in hotel rooms. Her pimp may be waiting outside for her in his car or having a drink in a bar nearby, but that doesn't help her when she finds herself locked in a room alone with a man determined to hurt her for his own pleasure. In some instances a pimp may even intentionally set up a prostitute with a violent customer as a punishment for in some way having disobeyed him.

If a prostitute is arrested, she also has no guarantee that her pimp will act immediately to secure her release. Often her freedom may depend on her pimp's mood as well as on his financial situation at the moment. If he doesn't have immediate access to sufficient funds for her bail, or if he is occupied procuring another female for his stable, he may ignore her call for help from the police precinct. If on the other hand, he needs her earnings immediately, he may quickly arrange for release.

It is nearly impossible for a woman who is involved with a pimp to have control over her earnings. The money she makes prostituting herself is usually not her own to spend as she wishes. Often she immediately gives most or all of it to the pimp. Her pimp will designate where she works as well as how many hours a day she'll spend on the street. He also sets the amount of money that she needs to earn before coming home. If a pimp is angry or annoyed at a prostitute, or even if he just wishes to reinforce his power over her, he may threaten to "pimp her hard" or raise the daily amount of money that she's required to earn.

Once a pimp has a young woman firmly under his control, he may use her to recruit other women for him as well. To encourage her to help him, the pimp will usually assure her that the new women will not be a threat to her because she will always be his "main woman." He may tell her that he could never really love anyone but her.

Often a pimp will tell a young woman that the other women will be like her sisters and that her life will be easier because there will be others to share in earning the family's income. The pimp will try to convince the girl that part of her obligation and responsibility to him entails actively recruiting other girls. Once a new girl is brought into the picture, the pimp's routine of befriending her, seasoning her, and then turning her out on the street is again initiated.

The forms of youth's sexual exploitation by adults may seem limitless. At times children have been turned into the prime commodity of organized business ventures that are adept at the sale of young flesh for high profits. Such establishments may include peep shows, strip bars, and prostitution rings disguised as escort services. These businesses may be run by men, women, or even seemingly middle-class couples or families. Sheila, an attractive seventeen-year-old runaway from Detroit described her experiences as an escort service's call girl this way:

"On my sixteenth birthday, I officially quit school. I told my parents that I wanted to leave home and that I would support myself in the city. My parents and I had been fighting a lot and finally I just left and went to Detroit. I looked older than my age so I did find a job—as a clerk in a warehouse. I can't describe the drudgery of it all. I had to work forty hours a week, broke two nails on my first day there, and after all that, I barely made enough money to meet my expenses.

"I was paying almost all I earned to share a tiny one-room apartment with three other girls. There was one girl down the hall whose name was Randy with whom I had become friendly. She seemed to live so well. She had great clothes and a big apartment of her own. I couldn't imagine how she did it. It was obvious that she didn't have any steady employment, but she sometimes hinted at being in the entertainment business. But one day when I asked her to tell me more about the entertainment business she was in, Randy came right out with the truth. In fact, she didn't even seem embarrassed about it. I remember that I had asked whether she sang or was a dramatic actress.

Randy simply smiled at me, squeezed my hand and answered, 'No, silly girl, I just entertain men.' She didn't have to say any more. Everything became crystal-clear immediately.

"I had sometimes daydreamed about becoming a call girl. I had read Xavier Hollander's book *The Happy Hooker,* and it all seemed so easy and exciting. First class travel, expensive furs, and lovemaking with handsome men who adored you.

"Randy said she made lots of money as a sort of fancy call girl for an escort service, and she offered to help me break into the business. I decided to go along with it. The woman who ran the service gave Randy a fee for bringing me to her. As Randy was my sponsor, she also received a portion of my earnings during my first month there.

"We were required to work four hour shifts during which we had to remain either in the service's townhouse or by a telephone. Some girls wore beepers. We had the choice of going to the customer's home or hotel room or of working out of the service's townhouse. In any case, we had to give the house half of our earnings for the referral. So in order to live well, you had to work a lot of hours.

"We girls were fined if we put on weight, fined a dollar a minute if we were late, and we had to pay the house one hundred dollars if we missed a day of work. They also charged us for lots of little extras, like using their soap and paper towels. The glamour and freedom that Randy appeared to have was just a front.

"The girls who worked for the house explained that it was too dangerous to try to work out on your own. The escort service that employed us looked like a legitimate business—it was incorporated and listed in the yellow pages. Supposedly, we only provided companionship for male clients, but our services were always extended beyond that.

"Still, the escort service served as a front for us, which tended to lessen police busts. In addition, the service was also supposed to screen our dates, so that we wouldn't end up with a sick violent customer who really wanted to hurt us. But it didn't always happen that way.

"Those who ran the service were more interested in making money than in protecting us, so if the price was right they tended to be more lenient in their screening. After all, we risked our lives, not them. Soon after I had begun working there, I learned that a little less than two years before, one of the girls had had her throat cut. And while I was with the service another girl became brain damaged after being severely beaten by a violent customer.

"I guess that I'd been naive about what prostitutes actually did. I thought that you just had straight sex. But men who want straight sex don't usually seek out prostitutes. Sex is too readily available for that. It's always those who want more from a girl who find us. Something that many women are unwilling to do.

"Most of the girls with whom I worked agree that there is a lot of unpleasantness involved in what we do. And remember, we were the classy call girls. I thought that the girls working the streets would have a hard time of it, but not us.

We were supposed to be leading the glamorous life.

"Randy had told me that most of the customers were really cute guys, but that was almost never so. Many of the men were considerably older than us and were overweight. Some had bad breath, others had body odor, and I soon became aware of the fact that just because a man has money doesn't mean that he's necessarily into cleanliness and personal hygiene.

"Several of the men were so filthy, that most of the girls actually dreaded being with them. But who we went with was determined by which girl the customer selected. We had no choice in the matter. Once we were chosen, we were not permitted to refuse.

"Whenever I got one of those smelly guys, I used to run into the shower and scrub my body as hard as I could to get his stink off me. But no matter how long I remained in the shower, it never seemed to work well enough. I just couldn't really feel clean doing what I was doing. And as if that weren't enough, I had to pay the service to have the sheets laundered as well.

"Before long I began to wish that I'd never been born. I always felt ashamed and sickened by what I did. I kept waiting for things to change, but they never did. There's nothing glamorous about prostitution once you've actually done it."

Chad—Age 17

My father abandoned my Mom and me when I was only four years old. As we had no money, we moved into my grandfather's house. My mother had never gotten along very well with her father, but she always said that we really had no choice since we'd be able to live there for free. But as it turned out, it wasn't free at all. I had to pay for our room and board with my body.

Shortly after my fifth birthday, my grandfather began sneaking into my room at night to molest me. I remember that it hurt awfully and that he used to clasp his hand over my mouth in order to muffle the sound of my cries. The pain and fear of these experiences dominated my life, and I came to really hate my grandfather. Whenever I heard him coming up the stairs to my room, I'd quickly hide under the bed and hold my breath hoping that he wouldn't find me. But he always did. He'd drag me out from under the bed, throw me down on the mattress, and use me.

My grandfather's visits to my room continued throughout my early childhood. I never said a word to anyone about what was going on. By the time I was six years old my hostility toward my grandfather must have really begun to show because my mother was always scolding me for my lack of warmth toward Grandpa. She constantly reminded me that we were dependent on her father for the roof over our heads and the food in our mouths. My mother warned that I was not to do anything to upset him. So at the age of six I came to feel responsible for the lives of both my mother and myself. And I tried to go on living with the feeling of horror that swept through my small body every time my grandfather put his hands on me.

I was seven when my grandfather began selling me to his friends for a dollar. By the time I had turned nine, he was willing to accept fifty cents for me. Although I had attempted to leave home on several occasions before, at eleven I ran away for good. My grandfather had already turned me into a prostitute, and I couldn't stomach him any longer. I knew that I could make more on my own. I felt that I'd be able to survive alone, and if I couldn't, at that point I felt so bad about myself, that it just didn't matter.

Home
Sweet Home

THE HOME SITUATION IN WHICH CHAD was raised is not untypical of the family lives of adolescent prostitutes. Often these young people grow up in families characterized by instability and change. A study by researcher Donald M. Allen published in the *Archives of Sexual Behavior* indicates a high frequency of broken homes among teenage male prostitutes, which were characterized by a lack of affection and communication. Allen found that only eighteen of the ninety-eight young males in his study came from a cohesive family environment in which both parents were "reasonably effective." In the vast majority of cases, there generally tended to be poor relationships among the various family members. According to Allen, "the parents, almost always the fathers, were either not present or present but nonsupportive or unstable. Disinterest, aloofness, hostility, and rejection were in one form or another continually registered towards the youth from his earliest years onward."

Available research data also suggests that both

young male and female prostitutes tend to have poorer relationships with their fathers than with their mothers. In a study for the National Institutes of Mental Health, researcher Mimi H. Silbert found that thirty-two percent of the female prostitutes in her sample reported a positive relationship with their mothers, while only nineteen percent acknowledged a comparably good relationship with their fathers.

Research conducted by the Huckleberry House, a center for runaways, yielded similar results. Almost half of the adolescents who had engaged in prostitution expressed negative feelings toward their fathers, whereas only ten percent pinpointed difficulties in their relationships with their mothers.

However, it may be interesting to note that even when young female prostitutes admitted having an unsatisfactory relationship with their father, many persisted in longing for his attention and approval. Numerous psychotherapists working with these young people have found that an extremely common feature of juvenile female prostitutes is a relentlessly strong attachment to their fathers. This has held true even in instances in which the father does not merit or even desire such an attachment.

Many adolescent prostitutes, both male and female, have had a number of different caretakers throughout their formative years. From a very early age on, many have been shifted from one living arrangement to another. Some have simply gone back and forth from various institutions and foster homes for as long as they can remember. A

41

number have been out on the street for a substantial part of their youth. Truancy and school problems have also been identifiable factors in their backgrounds.

Jerry's life is representative of this pattern. After his parents' divorce, Jerry lived with his mother, who unfortunately died of cancer when Jerry was only twelve years old. At this point Jerry went to live with his older brother for a while. After numerous squabbles over space and authority, Jerry left his brother's residence to live with some older male friends. He had just turned fourteen.

During this period, Jerry made a half-hearted attempt at remaining in school, but he felt unable to function successfully in an academic environment and within months simply stopped attending. At this point, Jerry was introduced to prostitution by the friends with whom he had been staying.

After learning all he could about it, Jerry actively began prostituting himself. He moved in with one of his steady customers for about five months. Following their breakup, he was subsequently arrested on the street for hustling.

Finally Jerry's case came to the attention of the court system. Jerry was assigned a social worker who placed him in a youth residence. Unhappy there, he moved back in with his brother who had agreed to be legally responsible for Jerry's welfare. But within six months Jerry ran away and struck out on his own again. To support himself, he sold his body for whatever price he could get. Jerry was sixteen years old at the time.

The homes from which adolescent prostitutes are spawned tend to be abusive environments. Many of these young people have reported that while at home they were abused by one or more household members. Often a mother, father, stepparent, or even older brother or sister may take part in the young person's degradation.

At times, the girls and boys were repeatedly beaten with fists, electrical cords, or leather straps. In a study conducted by Sivan E. Caukins and Neil R. Coombs published in *The American Journal of Psychotherapy,* it was found that the presence of "authoritarian" and "punitive" fathers was noted in the backgrounds of a significant number of adolescents who eventually became prostitutes. Numerous young prostitutes have claimed that leaving their homes and becoming active in "the life" was precipitated by recurring physical abuse.

Emotional abuse is often a common element within these home settings as well. At times, parents and other household members have been extremely destructive in their interactions with these young people. In many instances, scapegoating and humiliating the teenager may become an inherent part of everyday family life.

A number of adolescent male prostitutes have reported that adverse family reactions to their homosexuality resulted in their leaving home and eventually turning to prostitution as a means of survival. One young man revealed that his stepmother persuaded his father to throw him out of the house when the boy confided to her that he thought he might be a homosexual. She had two of her own sons living with them in the family, and she feared that he might corrupt her boys.

When another young man told his father that he had had a homosexual experience, his father told all the boy's friends as well as notified his high school teachers. He also took away the boy's car, which had been a recent birthday gift, and grounded his son until further notice.

The boy was so humiliated by his father's actions that he felt too ashamed to face anyone. He ran away from home. Once on his own with no source of income, he turned to prostitution and drug dealing.

It is not uncommon for adolescent prostitutes of either sex to have at some point in their lives been abandoned by their parents. Often single parents have felt too emotionally or financially burdened by their offspring and have placed the young child with relatives or in a state residential facility. In more traumatic instances, a parent has simply not returned home or has left a very young child in a public area.

One young man described his experience this way: "Sometimes my Mom and Dad were together, sometimes they weren't. Whenever they separated, I usually lived with my mother. At times I did the best I could for myself alone. I've sort of been living on and off the streets since I was eleven years old.

"Shortly after my fifteenth birthday, my mother threw me out for good. Actually, it was she who left. My mother simply announced that she'd be going off to live with her new boyfriend, and she didn't think that having a teenage boy hanging around the house would enhance her image in his eyes. So she just packed up her things and moved out. The last thing she said to me was, 'Good luck, kid. You're old enough to make it on your own now.'

"At this point I had no idea how she expected me to make it on my own. I didn't even know how I could scrape together enough money to pay the next month's rent for our apartment. I thought about getting in touch with my father, but we had lost contact with him years before, and I didn't know how to find him. My mother wouldn't even give me her new address or telephone number because she was afraid that I might intrude on her life.

"So as it turned out, I had to make a new start for myself as well. I was young and good-looking, and at first I was kind of amazed that people would pay money to sleep with me. My mother had always made me feel so worthless.

"Yet now customers were paying me to stay with them. All I had to do was to please them sexually. The hardest part was learning to live with all the shame, hate, and disgust I came to feel for myself. Still, at the time, I didn't see a lot of other choices open to me."

Sexual abuse prior to entering "the life" is another common component in the histories of both male and female teen prostitutes. Research conducted by the Huckleberry House Project estimates that at least ninety percent of all female adolescent prostitutes have been victims of sexual abuse. Often the sexual abuse of these children tends to be of long duration. Several female incest victims included in the study were first sexually abused between the ages of six and eight with the incest continuing until they ran away as young teenagers.

The research also seems to indicate that most adolescent prostitutes had their first sexual experience at an unusually early age. One seventeen-year-old prostitute stated that she had been sexually molested by her babysitter when she was little more than a toddler. A young male prostitute had been forcibly raped by his stepfather after the man had picked him up at school following his first day in kindergarten. Some teenage prostitutes have reported that they had been sexually abused from the time they were three or four years old.

In addition, an overwhelming number of adolescent prostitutes have been sexually abused as children by more than one adult. In one study, young prostitutes had been sexually abused prior to the age of ten by an average of two adults each. In numerous instances, physical force had been used against the victim. Many of these young people had been forcibly held down, slapped or beaten, or threatened with a weapon.

In other instances, the young victims were emotionally coerced, being told either that the sexual abuse was actually a demonstration of love or that it was their duty to do whatever was asked of them. In incestuous relationships involving fathers and their daughters, often the young girls were constantly reminded by their fathers that a good girl should want to please her Daddy.

Although both male and female adolescent prostitutes come from varied backgrounds and income levels, there is recent evidence to suggest that a significant number of them have middle-class backgrounds. In her study for the National Institutes of Mental Health entitled "Entrance Into Juvenile Prostitution," researcher Jennifer James found that a large number of adolescent female prostitutes frequently came from middle-class and even affluent homes. Many of the girls' parents had college educations, and a substantial number were professionals. However, in spite of their socioeconomic status, problematic family relationships still existed within these homes.

Statistically, the majority of both male and female prostitutes are Caucasian. Blacks make up the second largest racial group in which minors are involved in prostitution. Police reports and statistics gleaned by social service agencies indicate that Native American and Hispanic youths sometimes engage in prostitution, and reports of juvenile Asians becoming active in prostitution are still rare.

Pete—Age 16

You certainly wouldn't think of my childhood as something out of a movie, unless of course it was a horror film. I don't even remember my mother. She ran out on my Dad and me before I was two years old. For a time, my father and I moved in with his mother. My grandmother was the only person that I can remember as ever being kind to me. She used to bake chocolate chip cookies and sew colorful felt puppets with button eyes for me to play with.

But my grandmother died of cancer when I was five, and then things at our house really took a turn for the worse. My father had always had a drinking problem, but I guess that losing both his wife and his mother was more than he could handle. He began to go on long drinking binges, and whenever this happened, it was impossible to talk to him for days. My father was really mean whenever he was drunk. He'd yell at me and call me all kinds of names. I remember how he'd always blame me for his bad luck. After he lost his job, he started beating me with his belt.

As things worsened I felt I had to escape from that house. I had never really done well in school, and I didn't have many friends there. I wound up cutting class a lot and spending more and more time on the streets. There was a man about my father's age in our area, who ran a ladies' house of prostitution. His name was Bob, and I think that he liked young boys because he took an immediate interest in me. He bought me some new clothes and a bike, and perhaps best of all, he always had time to listen to me.

Our friendship grew, and within a few weeks I ended up in bed with him. I knew that we weren't going to have a permanent thing together, because Bob was married and had four young children. Still, Bob promised that we'd be good friends and that he'd always be there for me.

I saw Bob about three times a week for a while. Then one day he mentioned to me that he occasionally got requests for very young boys from clients who frequented his business. Bob asked if I were interested, adding that there'd be good money in it for me.

At first I felt hurt that Bob wanted to sell me that way. I knew that he was married, but I thought that there was something special between us and that in his own way Bob loved me. Still, I needed money badly. My father had nothing left to give me, and there usually wasn't any food in our house.

I figured that working for Bob wouldn't be that rough since my relationship with him had already groomed me for having sex with men. But I was wrong. It was bad; in fact, it was horrible. The men I was now with had no feeling for me and used me as if I weren't a human being. They called me names, degraded me, and made me do terrible things with them.

To make matters worse, about ninety percent of the money I earned went to Bob and the house. When I spoke to Bob about the split, it was as if our "friendship" had never existed. He simply said, "Too bad, kid, but that's the way it goes. If you can get a better deal elsewhere, go ahead. I won't try to stop you. There's plenty of others out there who'd be happy to replace you."

I felt angry and betrayed, and I decided to act on Bob's suggestion. By then I had learned all that I needed to know about prostitution, and I figured that there wasn't anything to keep me at home, certainly not Bob or my father. So I headed for the streets of Chicago to go into business for myself.

In the end, I don't think that it matters whether you're with a house or working out on your own, selling yourself still makes for a lousy stinking life. I lived with this one older client for about eighteen months, and I guess that he treated me well enough, but I knew that I wouldn't be able to stay with him for very much longer. He was so jealous and possessive that he wouldn't allow me to have any close friends or to even go out alone for that matter. He kept telling me that I would leave him. And after a year and a half that's just what I did.

I was out on my own again, and sometimes I feel as though thousands of men bought my body. And then I got sick. It had to have happened sooner or later. I guess that I had become depressed and wasn't screening customers too carefully. I knew that you were supposed to check them for VD, but I'm not really sure that I knew exactly what I was looking for anyway.

First I had this really disgusting syphilitic chancre sore. From that point on things really went downhill for me healthwise. The syphilis was soon followed by hepatitis and compounded by a severe case of gonorrhea. I was out of commission sexually and in a great deal of physical discomfort.

I didn't know where to turn. I was scared to go to one of those free public health clinics because I knew that they'd ask a lot of questions about my sexual contacts. According to the law, everyone you've been with has to be notified to insure that he receives medical treatment. After a physical examination, the doctors would be able to tell that I'd had homosexual sex, and if they realized that I was a prostitute, I was afraid that they'd contact the police. I was also scared to go to a private doctor because I didn't know whom I could trust not to report me.

I went back to the older man whom I had lived with to ask for his help, but he threw me out. He said that I was dirty and that he didn't want any part of me. He wouldn't even allow me to use the toilet. At this point, I felt desperate and alone, so I swallowed my pride and contacted Bob.

Seeing Bob felt a little awkward at first, but in no time at all I managed to blurt out my story to him. As always, Bob knew what to do and acted promptly. He had me seen and treated by a private physician who treats all of Bob's prostitutes. The doctor cured me and didn't report my case to the authorities.

After that I really didn't feel quite ready to go out and face it all again by myself. Bob sensed this and offered me another opportunity to work for him. This time I wouldn't actually have to prostitute myself very often. Bob noted that at sixteen I had lost the desirability that belongs to the nine-to eleven-year-olds.

51

I knew that what he said was true. Now my task would be to recruit the really young ones for Bob.

It turned out to be easy enough. All I had to do was to hang out near the playgrounds and video game arcades. Lost kids in trouble are easy to find. Most of the young boys were anxious to take advantage of my "help." Bob always supplied me with enough money to buy them a hamburger and loan them a few dollars. Besides, it really didn't cost him anything because he eventually deducted these expenses from the boys' first earnings.

I didn't like what I was doing. In fact, sometimes I felt like an animal. But whenever I wanted to stop I'd remind myself that there weren't a lot of available alternatives. It was either them or me on the street, and I felt that I had to save myself.

Where
the Boys Are

THE STORY OF THE HOUSTON, TEXAS, mass murders that shocked America broke in August of 1973. Three active sadists had brutally tortured and murdered twenty-seven young boys. As the authorities suggested that others besides the twenty-seven youngsters identified had been killed, the incident became widely known as the single largest mass murder in our nation's history. It was later discovered that at least eleven of the murdered youths had been boy prostitutes.

Although man-boy prostitution has existed for many years in America, the Houston murders were the first public acknowledgment that adult males were paying young boys for sex. Initiation into the world of prostitution tends to differ for adolescent males and females. Boys are often introduced to "the life" by older friends who have engaged in prostitution themselves. In addition, certain locales that tend to attract large throngs of adolescent boys often serve as ripe hunting grounds for potential customers.

Popular locations for male teen prostitution may include parks, beaches, bars, hotels, public toilets, and video game arcades. At times, an experienced young prostitute need only look visibly approachable in order to solicit his clientele. In some instances, a young man's first encounter with prostitution may occur almost inadvertently. He may be approached by an experienced customer who will sell him on the idea.

Greg, an attractive sixteen-year-old from California spent many of his summer days swimming and surfing with his friends at Venice Beach. A recent high school dropout, Greg had tried to find work on a number of occasions, but as yet nothing he wanted had turned up. So at the moment, Greg spent most of his time either lifting weights at the local gym or lolling at the beach.

Late one afternoon while Greg was hitchhiking back from the beach, a thirty-seven-year-old male computer programmer stopped to offer Greg a ride. The two struck up a conversation, and it wasn't long before the driver suggested to Greg that he might wish to earn a few dollars. Greg, who had been staying with friends after having left home, had almost no money left. He quickly agreed.

The two stopped off at a motel along the road. During the time they spent together the computer programmer confided to Greg that he was married and the father of two young daughters. He paid Greg in cash, making it clear that they would never see one another again. Greg had experienced casual sex with men before, but he had never been paid for it. Now for the first time he realized that his good looks were salable.

For the next two years Greg engaged in prostitution to support himself. At times he described some of the things that he had to do as repulsive. To enable him to continue, Greg devised his own mind games to transport himself mentally from the situation. He claimed that while he worked he kept silently repeating to himself that in a few moments it would all be over. Greg felt that he could handle what he was doing—that is, until the night a customer he had picked up off the street carved his initials on Greg's back.

Young boys who prostitute themselves are called "chickens." While some cite having homosexual inclinations, others have stated that theirs is a heterosexual orientation. These boys claim that what they do is unconnected to their sexuality. They prostitute themselves for the money, nothing more. Men are simply their most willing customers.

In interviews, many young prostitutes have boasted of having learned how to secure high fees as well as of being able to extricate gifts and favors from their patrons. Although it is difficult to differentiate between a boy's genuine mastery of his situation and his perhaps defensive feelings about being exploited, a number of boys have stated that they always manage to retain control of the interaction between themselves and their customers. They stressed that it is they who manipulate their customers rather than the other way around.

Any young male who prostitutes himself will soon find that he has to quickly become familiar with the rules of the game. To survive, it is essential that he learn how to try to avoid violent customers as well as the police. He must become knowledgeable as to the best locations and times of the day for business. He will also have to become expert at approaching potential customers, encouraging customers to approach him, and at negotiating prices.

Kevin, a fifteen-year-old prostitute explains his entrance into prostitution: "I had a couple of older friends I knew were prostitutes. When I asked one of them what you had to do to get started, he told me that I just needed to stand around and look good and that it wouldn't be long before someone approached me. I remember that he told me that as we were riding home from the beach one day. At the time I was wearing cut-off jeans and a ripped yellow faded tee shirt. Realizing that I didn't have much of a wardrobe, I mentioned that I'd probably have to get some really nice clothes in order to pull this off. But my friend quickly corrected me, saying that I looked young and sexy in exactly what I was wearing, and that was what sold.

"My friend suggested that I just lean against a park bench, fence, or tree and concentrate on looking good. He added that it was sort of like posing for a picture. And he was right, when I tried it, that was just what it felt like. My friend also pointed out some good locations to work in. In addition, some of my first customers added to the learning process supplying their own tips and pointers."

The available research suggests that the vast

majority of adolescent boys who engage in prostitution do so either to meet their survival needs or to support a drug habit. The correlation between the illicit use of drugs and young male prostitution is particularly high.

Some claim that they use drugs while prostituting themselves for a pleasurable experience, while others cited that they needed to "get high" in order to go through with what they are doing. These boys stress that drugs help them to mask the frightening consequences of what could happen, as well as assist in distracting them from what some have described as the unsettling aspects of prostitution.

Steve, a sixteen-year-old former prostitute, who recently entered a drug rehabilitation program in New York City, described his experiences in this manner: "I don't think that I could have gone through with it time after time, if I hadn't been able to keep myself well supplied with Quaaludes. Quaaludes act as a real strong downer, and if I was going out on the street to hustle, I always needed something to calm me down.

"I used to get nervous just thinking about it. There are a lot of violent guys out there, and there's no telling what they could do to you. You could be tortured, cut up, or even killed. And you're taking that risk for the chance to earn thirty-five or fifty dollars. I don't think that I could do it with a clear head.

"After being out there for a while, you really start to feel lonely and apart. The people whom you are supposedly 'making love to' treat you like dirt. After all, you're nothing more than something that they've bought and paid for. You're an object for them to do with as they wish.

"Before you even realize what's happening to you, all these feelings become connected with sex. It becomes difficult to have a decent relationship outside of your work. I found it particularly hard to trust anyone. I couldn't shake the feeling that everybody in my life wanted to use me for one thing or another. I felt a lot of anger at my customers for what they were doing to me as well as rage at myself for having allowed this to have happened to my body and my mind. And I just couldn't seem to separate these feelings from my personal life.

"Drugs and alcohol help to block out all the bad feelings. You need something, or I think you'd go crazy out on the streets. Your head gets so messed up, that even your good friends can't help you, if by that time you've got any of those left. So you keep taking drugs, and before you know it, your drug habit worsens. Then you're stuck with a problem that's as bad as prostitution, and even harder to break from."

At times very young boys who are alone and inexperienced may be recruited to participate in sex rings. Although such rings are less financially profitable for them, some young people who lack the skills and confidence to survive alone on the street may initially be drawn into this type of arrangement. These boys literally live and work out of boy houses of prostitution. Often such operations have recruiters who actively travel from city to city to procure new merchandise for the brothel customers.

The recruiter will frequent runaway habitats in various cities promising food, shelter, and a chance not only to survive but also to make big money. To a desperate young runaway, who doesn't know where his next meal is coming from, it's an appealing offer. After befriending the boy and transporting him back to the brothel, the recruiter is once again on the road in search of new finds.

Many boy brothels are situated in private homes in quiet residential areas. Usually they exist inconspicuously within a community. One such young male prostitution ring was run out of a spacious and luxurious house on a tree-lined street in a small town in Westchester County, New York. There over twenty-five boys ranging in age from nine to fourteen were available for the customers' selection. The boys, who engaged in any sexual activity desired by the customer, could be had for between twenty-five and thirty dollars apiece. Of this amount each boy received five dollars plus room and board. They were expected to work seven days a week.

The prostitution ring continued to function until a neighbor began to notice an unusually heavy amount of man-boy traffic entering and leaving the house at odd hours of the day and night. The local police were notified, and after an adequate surveillance period the operation was raided and shut down.

However, organized boy prostitution continues to thrive in the United States as well as overseas.

59

For the right sum, clients can secure youthful pornography and young males. Many boy sex rings secure patrons through classified ads in newspapers and magazines as well as by word of mouth. Some rings claim that they can deliver a boy of any height, build, and age desired by the consumer. Orders placed over the telephone may require using various codes to evade possible discovery through phone taps. Using the pretext of ordering wine, a customer who asks for a ten-year-old full-bodied wine is in reality requesting a firmly built ten-year-old boy.

In many instances a direct connection exists between boy prostitution and child pornography. A photographer may initially approach a young boy on the pretext of asking the boy to model sportswear for him. Attracted by the high model's fee offered, the boy may readily agree. However, once in the photographer's studio, the job will usually entail other facets of modeling. For example, the boy may be asked to model underwear, pose nude, and eventually do sex shots. The sequence of events may take place over a period of days or weeks. A boy who feels squeamish about engaging in homosexual activities will be told that what he's doing isn't real—he is simply on an acting assignment. Once the boy can begin to accept his actions psychologically, he may be assigned an even more challenging acting role—that of being a full-time prostitute.

One large-scale California kiddie porn operation was broken up following the arrests of a local high school teacher and a free-lance photographer who together had run the boy sex ring. It was estimated that over three hundred young boys had been used in pornographic films and photographs over a ten-year period with over fifteen thousand photographs alone confiscated during the police raid.

The free-lance photographer had had the assignment of taking yearbook pictures for a local high school, and he along with the teacher had recruited the boys directly from their classes. The police bust came when one of the students accompanied his friend to the teacher's home to observe a photography session and determine if he wanted to become a model. The boy decided that he wanted no part of it and went home to report what was taking place to his parents. In turn, the boy's parents notified the police.

There is a flush market in the United States for kiddie porn featuring both boys and girls. Whenever either sex is involved, these activities generally serve as one of the many direct routes to child and adolescent prostitution.

Perhaps one of the most disturbing available texts that deals with child prostitution is not at all a pornographic work but rather a thirty-two page travel guide entitled *Where the Young Ones Are.* The book contains no information other than the listings of three hundred and seventy-eight places in fifty-nine cities of thirty-four states where children and adolescents may be found for the purpose of prostitution.

The book's preface states: "We have through representatives throughout the country sought to provide an accurate listing of where the young action is today. All listings have been checked and verified. However, the possibility of error does exist due to the human interpretation of such words as 'young,' 'active,' and the like."

The text also includes this "message of caution" to its readership: "The age of consent varies between state and state. Check your state and the states you travel through for the current status. Also, many communities have numerous ordinances for loitering, curfew violation, and other activities you might engage in. Protect yourself and the person you would be with. Although many times you may be morally right, you can be legally wrong. Stay happy and free to enjoy *Where the Young Ones Are.*"

The book contains only location listings—no photographs or pornographic material of any sort is included. Over 50,000 copies have been sold to people who had no other reason for purchasing the volume than to find out "where the young ones are." A frightening reality, but one that exists nonetheless.

Male adolescents who become adept at prostitution may become "call boys." Call boys generally do not work off the streets but rather secure customers through advertising or by working with an agency. They usually run their ads under "Personal Services" columns in appropriate newspapers and magazines. They may offer something like home massages or photographic modeling. There are also "Personals," which may be small ads specifically taken out to attract adults who desire relationships with younger boys.

In some instances, customers may be referred through other call boys. To be successful, a call boy must keep records of his clients' phone numbers and preferences. He must become adept at being able to cultivate a steady stream of customers while maintaining his emotional distance in the course of their interaction.

Men who desire sexual liaisons with young boys are called "chickenhawks." Those who seek out the services of young male prostitutes tend to be between thirty and fifty-five years of age. They are usually Caucasian and come from varied social and educational backgrounds. Some are married with families, others are single. Although at times women have purchased sex from male children and adolescents, the vast majority of clients are men.

Acts of teen male prostitution often occur in the customer's home or car, rather than in a hotel. In some instances, a young male prostitute may tend to avoid working out of hotels, as an adolescent boy entering a hotel room with an older man might immediately arouse suspicion.

Even a young call boy, who is able to retain customers successfully, encounters many difficulties with which he must contend. The risks of arrest, handling violent customers, or of contracting venereal disease are always present. In addition, many young prostitutes find it exceedingly difficult to live with the humiliation that is inherent in their work.

An adolescent prostitute also faces barriers that beset all minors who attempt to live on their own. For example, few adolescent prostitutes have their own apartments, although many wish to have them. Instead, they are usually forced to settle for short-term living arrangements, often with customers or friends. To secure an apartment of his own, the young person would have to provide proof to the landlord that he is of age to sign a lease as well as offer evidence of a steady source of income. He simply can't put "call boy" down as his occupation on the apartment application.

Both male and female teen prostitutes tend to have similar attitudes regarding money as well as corresponding spending habits. Often seeming proud of the fact that they are capable of earning large sums of money in their profession, they are quick to report exceedingly high incomes when interviewed.

However, despite their ability to generate significant earnings, these youths rarely retain very much of what they earn. A study conducted by researchers Robert W. Deisher, Greg Robinson, and Debra Boyer published in *Pediatric Annals* revealed that few adolescent prostitutes accumulate any savings or substantial assets and that the vast majority have no form of bank account whatsoever. What is earned, is usually quickly spent. The greatest outlays of cash are generally for drugs, clothing items, or entertainment.

In fact, these young people rarely have very much money on their person. In one study a group of young male prostitutes were asked to count the money in their pockets at the time of the interview. More than half of the boys had less than one dollar, while only a few possessed more than five dollars. Yet despite this fact, many young men initially enter prostitution with the dream of becoming wealthy.

A New Country/
An Old Profession

ADOLESCENT PROSTITUTION IS NOT A new phenomenon. Prostitution has existed in America ever since our country's beginnings. And although then, as now, prostitutes varied in age, a premium has always been placed on youth. The younger the girl, the more desirable she was considered.

In early Western boomtowns, the saloonkeepers were generally responsible for selecting and transporting young girls from the East to work as prostitutes in their establishments. After arriving each girl had to live and work out of a small space known as a "crib." In actuality, a crib was little more than a tiny house about one third the size of an actual room. In addition to being poorly paid for their services, the girls were required to pay the saloonkeeper a fee for the use of the crib.

Young prostitutes on the frontier did not have an easy time of it. Besides the prostitutes who worked in the saloons, others labored in rough mining camps, or traveled in medicine shows, in carnivals, or with acting troops. There were also private caravans of prostitutes who rode with the army or braved the vigorous trails to work at the particularly lucrative gold camps. Although some of the girls might have hoped to gain their share of the riches, this rarely occurred. Prostitutes in the early West generally died quite young and very poor.

Variations in status existed among these young prostitutes as well. Prostitutes who were also dance hall girls and singers were held in higher esteem than the girls who followed the army troops or worked out of the crude "cathouses" that had begun to spring up. A saloon girl was considered more desirable, as she provided both entertainment and "companionship" for the male patrons.

However, life was still difficult for these young women, and many took their lives before reaching their eighteenth birthday. At the first signs of aging, it was customary for saloon girls to be sent to work in the cathouses of the town's red-light district. A girl was generally considered "older" once she turned sixteen. Numerous prostitutes chose to die rather than endure this humiliation.

In fact, an overwhelming number of prostitutes both in the saloons and on the caravans throughout the West committed suicide. Often the girls were supplied with morphine and other drugs. They were given the drugs to serve as an incentive to work as well as to insure their continued dependency. At times, when their personal pain became too great, some girls took deliberate overdoses. This form of escape became so common among young prostitutes of the West that it was called the Morphine Route.

The vast majority of these girls had not turned to prostitution willingly. In many instances they had been forced into the work by personal circumstances or by extreme financial necessity. In 1854 a medical doctor named William W. Sanger questioned over two thousand young women to learn their reasons for becoming involved in prostitution. His results were later tabulated and published in a wide study of prostitution at the time. Among the leading causes cited by the girls were:

Destitution
Seduction and abandonment
Ill-treatment from parents and relatives
Bad company
Persuasion by other prostitutes
Sexual violation
Seduction on board emigrant ships

As new immigrant groups arrived in the West it was not uncommon for the young females to become involved in prostitution. Often being poor as well as victims of racial or ethnic prejudice, these very young girls became especially vulnerable targets. Some were even brought West against their will, as was the case with young Chinese prostitutes in the 1850's.

By 1854, prostitution and gambling were among the major business enterprises in San Francisco, with the vast majority of prostitutes being young Chinese girls. These girls had been brought to the area from China, where they had either been purchased or been kidnapped by agents working for San Francisco dealers.

An article in the *San Francisco Chronicle* (December 5, 1868) stated:

"The particularly fine portions of the cargo, the fresh and pretty females who come from the interior, are used to fill special orders from wealthy merchants and prosperous tradesmen. A very considerable portion are sent to the interior under charge of special agents, in answer to demands from well-to-do miners and successful vegetable producers. Another lot of the general importation are examined critically by those desiring to purchase, and are sold into the 'trade' or to individuals ranging from $500.00 down to $200.00 per head, according to their youth and attractiveness. The refuse, consisting of the 'boat-girls' and those who come from seaboard towns, where they have had contact with white sailors, is sold to the proprietors of select brothels or are used in the more inferior dens of prostitution under the immediate control of the 'swell companies.' Those who are inflicted with disease, who suffer from the incurable attacks of Asiatic scrofula, or have the misfortune of possessing a bad temper, are used in this last manner mentioned."

The dealers had a brief contract drawn up between themselves and the girls. The purpose of these contracts was to assure the local authorities that the girls had come to this country of their own free will to work as prostitutes. The contract basically stated that the girl had promised to prostitute her body. Each girl was forced to sign one. If a girl refused, she would be systematically beaten and starved until she yielded. In addition, an overwhelming majority of these girls did not read English and had no idea what they were signing.

The contract also specified that if a girl was sick one day and unable to work, two days would be added to her contractual agreement. If she needed more than one sick day at a time, she'd be forced to prostitute herself for another month.

This clause served to keep the young women in a state of perpetual slavery. Since the girls were not permitted to work during their menstrual period, each was forced to take off a minimum of three days a month. Such mandatory absences insured that their contracts never expired. The young girls became locked into a vicious cycle.

The average "yellow slave," as these young Chinese prostitutes were referred to, usually did not survive for very long. In most houses of prostitution, the girls were not permitted to refuse a customer. This rule was enforced even if a customer showed visible signs of venereal disease. As the girls became infected and died, others were brought in to replace them.

Although not a great deal is known about them, there were young male prostitutes in San Francisco as well. The vast majority of these boys were runaways who had journeyed West in search of adventure.

Considered easy prey, they were often readily seduced by brothel syndicate agents. After gaining the boys' trust, the agents delivered them to boy houses of prostitution, where they were often abused by both the customers and the owners. An agent was given anywhere between one hundred and five hundred dollars for each boy delivered.

Child and adolescent prostitution existed in the East as well. In the late 1880's unscrupulous businessmen systematically introduced to the trade poverty-stricken girls and boys they found begging in the streets. One boy brothel in New York City known as The Golden Rule Pleasure Club dressed up young boy prostitutes to look like girls. Potential customers were taken on a tour of the club's basement, which was divided into cubicles. In each cubicle, a young boy who had been given a girl's name as well as dressed in girls' clothing sat waiting to be selected.

Although times have changed, in many ways prostitution has not. Thousands of unhappy young girls and boys are still prostituting themselves in a desperate effort to survive. Drugs and suicide are still an inherent part of prostitution's subculture. The faces may be different, but the pain is still the same.

Laurie—Age 15

I'll never forget how it happened. I had just turned fifteen, and as a birthday present my parents allowed me to drive down to West Virginia with my older sister Beth. Beth was going to take courses at the University of West Virginia that summer, and I had planned to spend a week or two visiting our aunt who lived near the campus.

My sister had just gotten a new car, and I thought that driving down and stopping at local spots along the way would probably be an unforgettable adventure. And as it turned out the experience was unforgettable, but for all the wrong reasons.

In any case, the first few days of our vacation were wonderful. We had allotted about a week for the trip, and it was fun driving along and sometimes stopping to spend the afternoon at a lake or to do some shopping and sightseeing. Each night we'd stay at a different motel, and if there wasn't a disco or night spot there, we always managed to find a desk clerk or bellboy who'd direct us to a fun place.

Technically, I was underage and wasn't allowed in establishments where liquor is served. But I looked older with my makeup on, and no one at the door ever asked for proof of age. This was my first vacation without my parents, and I was really anxious to have a good time.

Everything was going great until the evening that we stopped at a tavern in Maryland. It was a wonderful place, full of atmosphere, with a terrific band. But the best part of it all was that two of the handsomest guys I had ever seen had been dancing with Beth and me all evening and buying us beers. I never danced or drank so much before, and as the hours passed, I guess that I was beginning to feel a little dizzy. Dave, the guy I was with, suggested that we step out for a walk in the cool night air.

Being out of the hot smoky bar helped somewhat, and then Dave suggested that we go for a drive. He told me that he knew of this small tucked-away café where they served the best coffee and pecan pie in the state. It sounded like a good idea, but when I told him that I wanted to go back to the tavern to tell Beth where we were going, Dave tried his best to stop me. He said that Beth and his friend were probably out on the dance floor and that there was no need to interrupt them.

In any case, Dave promised to have me back before Beth even realized that I was gone. So I left without saying good-bye to my sister, all the while never imagining that I wouldn't see her again for almost six months.

The rest was more horrible than I can describe. Apparently, Dave, if that was his real name, had never had any intention of taking me out for coffee and pecan pie. I knew that something was wrong almost immediately as he drove onto the highway because I remembered that he had said the place we were going to was only a few miles away. When I questioned our route, he just said "Shut up, little sister," and slapped me so hard across the face that my nose started to bleed.

At that point I think that I began to realize what was happening and I felt sick to my stomach. I found myself crying hysterically. I just couldn't stop. And once again Dave simply said, "Shut up," and delivered another severe blow to my head. My ears stung and my jaw hurt, but I knew that I had to do something to help myself.

The car was going at about sixty miles an hour, but I felt that my only chance was to try to get out. Unfortunately Dave apparently anticipated my move. Just as my hand reached for the door handle, Dave grabbed my shoulder and pulled me toward him. Then he hit me so hard that I was knocked unconscious.

I don't know how long I was unconscious or how long we rode on that highway. I only remember that when I came to I was gagged and bound in the car's trunk. I knew that it was morning because when Dave opened the trunk the bright light hurt my eyes and glimmered on the long blade of the knife he used to cut the ropes that tied my limbs. As Dave lifted me out of the trunk, he gently pressed the knife against my throat and whispered only, "Behave."

Looking around me, I guessed that we were in a secluded area of sorts. There was only one large building, which looked like an inn with two smaller structures alongside of it. The inn was surrounded by a small plot of farmland and a dense wooded area for as far as you could see.

Standing in the yard was an overweight bald man who looked to be in his fifties. At his side was a short slender woman with graying hair of about the same age. When I stood up the man slapped

73

me across the backside, and said to Dave, "Now this is what I like. You finally brought me a real young one. She'll do just fine." The man took a large wad of bills from his back pocket, which he counted out and gave to Dave, while the woman took my hand and gently led me into the inn. I was too scared to say a word, but at that point I realized that I had just been sold.

*   *   *

As it turned out Laurie was held against her will and forced to prostitute her body. On numerous occasions, she was threatened as well as physically abused. After close to six months in captivity, Laurie was finally able to escape.

Sold to the
Highest Bidder

I N THE PUBLIC'S MIND FORCED PROSTI-
tution and traffic in sexual slavery for the most
part do not exist. Many people tend to view
"white slavery" as a phenomenon of the last century. Yet despite its scant coverage by the media,
sexual slavery still occurs. For many people, sexual slavery is a highly profitable business that is
widely conducted on an international level.
Hundreds of instances are reported annually, and
it's been estimated that many more go unre-
ported. According to the Interpol report entitled
"Traffic in Women: Recent Trends," "it may be
supposed that the number of cases of traffic in
women that never come to the attention of the authorities is quite high."

Sexual slavery may involve both young girls
and young boys. In instances in which males are
procured, the boys tend to be extremely young.
The means for procuring young males and females generally involves the use of various ploys.
The young people may be duped into believing
that they've won a free trip to Europe, or that a

75

kind but lonely gentleman with no family of his own wishes to take them with him on vacation for companionship. Or an advertisement may be run in a newspaper offering jobs as bar hostesses, dancers, or actors and actresses for theatrical troupes.

An ad was recently placed to recruit young American girls to dance in a ballet troupe that would supposedly tour Europe. However, once recruited and transported to foreign countries, the girls quickly realized that the dance group never existed. They were physically and sexually abused, kept under lock and key, and forced to prostitute themselves.

In such instances the young prostitutes' passports are immediately confiscated to prevent them from leaving as well as from proving their real identities. In some cases they are given false passports and identification. The end result is that captured children and adolescents may suddenly find themselves without money, a family, or a passport in a strange country where they are unable to either understand or speak the language.

In one such case a sixteen-year-old girl, who had quit high school and run away from home, answered an ad to display dogs at dog shows. At her interview three women drugged the girl by slipping a strong sedative into her soft drink. Having provided the drugged girl with a false passport, the women convinced the airline's staff that because of a serious illness the girl had to board the plane by stretcher. In this manner, they managed to transport her to West Germany.

Once securely under her kidnappers' control, the girl had initially resisted their demand that she prostitute herself. As a result she was threatened, beaten, and thrown down an iron staircase into a dank cellar. After several weeks of being tortured, the girl relented and went to work in the brothel. However, this girl was among the fortunate ones. She managed to escape and find an English-speaking person who took her to police headquarters.

There are prostitution rings throughout Europe that specialize in procuring young boys for traveling businessmen as well as for vacationing males. Some rings claim that for the right price, a customer may purchase the use of a good-looking boy between seven and thirteen years of age. The younger the boy, the higher the cost. In several instances, in which prostitution rings were disbanded by the authorities, it was discovered that a number of the boys had been kidnapped and forcibly held in the boy brothels.

Children and adolescents are often the victims of sexual slavery. Youth is perhaps among the most salable qualities in the world of prostitution. In many instances, the victims are runaway or throwaway young people. Even if a kidnapped young person has a concerned family, often their chances of locating the child are slim. But unfortunately, for many of the young people in sexual slavery, no one has ever tried to find them.

Community Response

JUVENILE AND ADOLESCENT PROSTI-
tutes exist on the edges of our society. Despite the fact that many Americans may
appear outraged over the reality that prostitution
involving minors exists, there are still few wide-
spread resources available for young people who
become entangled in this predicament.

Adult prostitution cases are generally handled
by police vice squads. In many instances, it may
not be immediately apparent that some of the individuals involved in these incidents are in fact
minors. Often these young people dress to look
older. Some have already acquired a worn look
from living on the street or from their use of
drugs. Others have been supplied with false identification in order to conceal their actual age.

Some vice squad officers may tend to view prostitutes more as criminals than as victims. This attitude may be reinforced by the reality that many
adolescent prostitutes pursue a lifestyle that often
leads them to become involved in illegal activities. It's not uncommon for young prostitutes to

engage eventually in petty theft, pickpocketing, and drug dealing in addition to other offenses.

Many of these teenagers, who were abused and neglected as very young children, may experience difficulties in relating to authority figures—especially to the police. At times their streetwise appearance combined with an almost insulting attitude toward regulations and authority may unfortunately serve to underscore a police officer's view of them as troublemakers. As a result, police intervention may take the form of arrest rather than a rehabilitative approach. The primary police objective may become that of removing young prostitutes from the streets with little thought given to helping these teenagers to change their lives.

Some law enforcement agencies have attempted to combat adolescent prostitution through the arrest of pimps, as pimps promote prostitution. However, bringing a pimp to trial is usually not an easy task. In order to prosecute a pimp, the prostitute involved must be willing to testify against him in court. Many young prostitutes are reluctant to do this. Some may still be emotionally involved with their pimp and therefore wish to protect him. If on the other hand, a girl has become disillusioned with her pimp, she may still hesitate to testify if she fears him.

In a number of progressive police departments such as those in Seattle and Minneapolis, officers have tried to befriend young female prostitutes by offering them emotional as well as residential support services in exchange for their testimony against their pimps. Although this tactic has proved successful in some instances, the odds are against the police as many pimps have been extremely violent in their retribution, and the young girls realize that it is unrealistic to expect indefinite police protection.

Usually the adolescent prostitute's customers are not arrested. The dearth of arrests in this area may reflect a long-standing law enforcement policy of generally not prosecuting a prostitute's patrons. In any case, in order to bring a customer to court, either a police officer must observe a person committing the criminal act or the prostitute must agree to testify against him. Either of these circumstances tends to be difficult to achieve.

Male adolescent prostitutes often fare especially poorly with law enforcement officials. Some police officers tend to have an indifferent attitude toward male prostitutes. Boys are often perceived as being less vulnerable than young girls and therefore as less deserving of help and attention. In addition, at times police agencies have experienced difficulties in recruiting officers to pose as customers with young male prostitutes in order to secure arrests. Some officers have expressed discomfort at even being touched casually in a sexual way by another male. When this type of work is required, many vice squad officers prefer soliciting adolescent female prostitutes for the purpose of arrest.

However, recent years have witnessed some attitudinal changes on the part of a select number of police agencies across the country. In some instances, special units within the police force itself are being created to specifically deal with the sexual exploitation of juveniles. Among the innovative police programs are those in Indianapolis, Los Angeles, Seattle, Washington, D.C., and Louisville, Kentucky. There are others in different parts of the country as well.

In these projects, the adolescent prostitute is regarded as a victim rather than as the perpetrator of a criminal act. In some instances, these units have attempted to shield the young persons from stigma by referring to each on the records only as "exploited child" or "missing child" rather than "runaway" or "juvenile prostitute."

In some jurisdictions, cases of this nature are investigated by a two-person team consisting of a police officer and a social worker. Often their findings may be reported to a citywide task force set up to deal with the problems of exploited youth. As a result, rather than being arrested, the young person may be offered some very much needed social services.

A number of areas have established unique centers within police precincts to serve as a clearinghouse for all information relating to juvenile sexual exploitation. These divisions may run staff training sessions on this issue for police officers and other personnel. Emphasis is placed on increased communication between community agencies and local law enforcement staff. In this manner, police officers are made aware of possible social service resources that might be made available to adolescent prostitutes.

In some municipalities new police programs have been designed to offer special assistance to very young prostitutes. This is extremely important as minors under the age of fourteen have been shown to be especially vulnerable to exploitation by both customers and pimps.

In addition to problems with the law, both male and female adolescent prostitutes usually must contend with a number of health problems. Perhaps the most common physical ailments involve venereal diseases or other illnesses that may at times be sexually transmitted, such as hepatitis.

Pregnancies have been noted as a problem for some young female prostitutes, while colds, sore throats, and the flu are frequently common for both sexes. In addition, as drug use is frequently high among adolescent prostitutes, drug related illnesses tend to result as well. The most common mental health problems that affect adolescent prostitutes include severe depression and a preoccupation with suicidal thoughts as well as actual suicide attempts. Often severe depression in adolescent prostitutes leads to a general lack of concern for their own physical health and the inevitable consequences of life on the street.

Many adolescent prostitutes have felt intimidated by traditional health care facilities and physicians. Although they may be in need of health services, prior negative experiences have often prevented them from receiving the necessary attention. According to Dr. Robert W. Deisher and his associates in his study entitled "The Adolescent Female and Male Prostitute" published in *Pediatric Annals,* the reason for their avoidance may be due to the fact that "they perceive medical personnel as authority figures representing general societal values which conflict with their personal characteristics and experiences on the street."

Often obtaining medical services at a traditional treatment center may prove especially difficult for young male prostitutes. A young male prostitute needing treatment for a venereal disease may be well aware of the fact that a physical examination will reveal his homosexual experiences. He may uneasily anticipate the physician's condemnation of his activities, whether or not this may actually prove to be the case. The boy may also be concerned that the doctor will suspect that he has been involved in prostitution after questioning him about the extent of his sexual contacts, and as a result, these young males often tend to defer treatment.

In addition, many adolescent prostitutes have only a limited knowledge of sexually transmitted diseases and of good health and hygiene practices. The vast majority of young prostitutes left home at an early age. In most cases, their formal education was interrupted, and their accurate knowledge of sexuality and venereal disease may be largely incomplete.

In many instances, most of what they know about sexual health was acquired on the street along with a good deal of misinformation on the subject. As a result, these young people may often be unaware of the early warning signs of some sexually transmitted diseases and may therefore delay seeking medical attention until the disease has progressed and more serious symptoms have surfaced.

A recent study conducted for the National Institutes of Mental Health demonstrated that female adolescent prostitutes also lacked adequate information on birth control practices. Often these young women did not have correct information on how to prevent pregnancy or were inconsistent in practicing birth control.

Even when adolescent prostitutes obtain medical assistance, health care professionals may find it difficult to complete adequate follow-up procedures in these cases. This problem may be due in part to the fact that life on the street may not always be conducive to taking medication on a prescribed schedule or to keeping scheduled medical appointments.

In recent years, some alternative medical facilities designed to better meet the health needs of adolescent prostitutes and others who have been exposed to street life have been created. Among these are the medical services offered by Covenant House in New York City, The Bridge Over Troubled Waters in Boston, the Lesbian and Gay Community Services Center in Los Angeles, the Red Door Clinic in Minneapolis, and the Pioneer Square Youth Services Clinic in Seattle.

For example, the Red Door is an alternative health care center, providing screening and treatment for venereal diseases, which has attempted to especially publicize its programs to male prostitutes in the area. Counseling for adolescent prostitutes involving the inherent dangers of life on the street is also available. The Pioneer Square Youth Services Clinic maintains a free medical facility for young people in downtown Seattle, where in addition to medical services and private counseling sessions, free seminars are available on such topics as adolescent pregnancy, prostitution, transexuality, and drug and alcohol abuse among others.

At one time or another many runaway youths who have turned to prostitution may find themselves in need of temporary shelter. In 1974 the federal government enacted the Runaway Youth Act, which made available federal funding to establish youth shelters for runaways. A number of these shelters now exist in communities across the country which provide emergency shelter, crisis counseling, and in some instances, medical assistance.

The problems faced by runaway shelters are twofold. As of yet there are still not sufficient shelters established to meet the needs of the numbers of young people out on the streets. However, even when such shelters exist, at times they may experience difficulty reaching the young people whom they seek to serve.

Some street youth may hesitate to avail themselves of help from these shelters, as many are generally distrustful of social service programs and fear that they may be either sent home to their families or reported to the authorities because of their involvement in illegal activities. At times female prostitutes have refused to use these shelters, because they're afraid that their pimp will learn of their whereabouts and realize that they are contemplating leaving him.

Lastly, many young people on the streets are aware that runaway programs are generally authorized to provide only temporary shelter and therefore can never be a permanent solution for a young person in need of a home. Adolescents with a long history of rejection often feel uneasy about becoming connected with a place and people who will only eventually try to help them find still another environment to adjust to.

Even in instances in which young people have effectively linked up with a social service agency and been placed in a long-term living facility, difficulties often still arise. Adolescent prostitutes often have numerous emotional problems, which they may unintentionally bring to each new situation.

Besides being homeless and prostitutes, these young people are usually undereducated and unskilled. Many have been both physically and emotionally abused as well as having had some involvement with drugs and/or alcohol. The vast majority of these girls and boys have a lengthy history of being in trouble with the law. Often these individuals unconsciously perpetuate a failure syndrome in which they allow their previous failures with social service agencies to influence their behavior negatively, even in a fresh situation.

It is sometimes difficult for a young person who has been on his or her own for some time to adjust to the rules and regulations inherent in any group-living situation. In some instances, even minor requirements such as adhering to curfews or taking one's turn doing the dishes have been viewed as too restrictive.

At times to retaliate or to prove to themselves as well as to the others that they are still in control, some young residents may openly and deliberately defy house rules. They may stay out on the street for a few days or sneak drugs into the residence. If such actions are repeated often enough and the young person doesn't immediately respond to counseling, that individual may find himself or herself expelled from the home and back out on the street.

One counselor at a group home in New York City explained, "We've only got two professional staff counselors on during any shift, and it's our responsibility to keep the home running effectively. We really try to help everybody, honestly. I can't tell you how hard we've worked with some of these kids. At times I've stayed up all night to comfort one or more of them.

"We give them as many chances as we possibly can, and then if they still can't fit in, they have to go. You see, there are a lot of kids whom we can help and who are doing okay here. But it isn't fair to anybody if some kids have to obey the rules and share the housework while others living among them refuse to do so. I wish that we could save everybody, but I have to be realistic. I know that we can't. So we have to pour the major portion of our time and energy into kids who at this point are ready to turn around their lives.

"The others are left to fend for themselves on the street, where they live and where, unfortunately, they sometimes die."

Marianne—Age 14

I can't remember a time when my mother didn't hit me. When I was very young if I cried for any reason at all, she'd slap me hard across the face saying, "You've got nothing to cry about. I'll give you something to cry about." Other times if I smiled or laughed, my mother would strike me as well and accuse me of ridiculing her. My mother didn't need a reason to beat me. My fate as a very young girl depended only on my mother's whims and how much she had had to drink that day.

According to my mother, I never did anything right. As I grew older, no matter how hard I tried, I was unable to please her. She was devilishly quick to point out a flaw in my behavior, which was usually almost immediately followed by the palm of her hand slamming hard against my head or the side of my face.

Looking back now, I think that my mother must have really hated herself. I was her daughter and I looked just like her, so maybe she treated me so badly because she felt that in some way I was an extension of her. I don't know for certain.

Although everybody was always commenting on how pretty I was, my mother seemed to need to put me down. She'd constantly say how ugly or fat I was, and she suggested that I walk around the house with a paper bag over my head so that she'd be spared looking at my face. Whenever I'd get all dressed up to go out with my friends, my mother would make a point of scorning me. She'd say that I was the worst-looking kid in the world and that my pretty girl friends made me look worse by comparison.

After hearing something like that, I usually wouldn't feel like going out anymore. My mother was filled with rage and a lot of it splashed over into my life. She made my everyday existence dreadful. I was forced to deal with her continual abuse, which in reality had very little to do with my actions. I had just become my mother's victim.

By the time I had turned thirteen, I felt that I had to leave home. To even call our apartment a home was a joke. I had never known my father, and if my mother had to be my only family, I thought that I'd be better off alone. A social worker later told me that sometimes when we get off to a painful start in life, without really realizing it, we help to continue our own misery. And I guess that's what I did for a long time. If you've always heard that you're worthless, you eventually come to believe it, and before you know it, you begin to treat yourself as badly as your parent did.

I became involved with a pimp. He was an older guy. I guess that at first I saw him as being somewhat charming and handsome. He had picked me up wandering around the streets and had nicknamed me his Angel Face. In any case, I hoped that he was somehow going to change my whole life with his love. That is until he began selling me right off the street to strange men and taking everything I earned. But I thought that, after all, it was just one more betrayal. The way my pimp had treated me sort of fit in with everything else that had ever happened in my life.

I always felt full of hopelessness. I led a life of

entering dark rooms with unknown men for money. When you're on the street, you have to live with a certain amount of fear and anxiety. A lot of young prostitutes are murdered every year. No one cares about these girls. They are somehow considered worthless; it's almost as if they weren't even human beings. These are the girls who live outside of respectable society. The girls who led secret lives with anonymous patrons. And as a result, their murders are nearly always impossible to solve.

I knew one girl who was even younger than me, whose body was found with over forty-seven stab wounds. Think about it—she was murdered by a sadist who had paid to make love to her. He was never caught, and for all we know he could still be out there buying us. And everytime I climb the dark hotel stairs with a new trick or get into a strange car, I know that I could be next.

Most of us take drugs of some sort to try to ward off what we feel, but nothing really works well enough. Nothing could. I know that everyday that I'm on the street, I'm taking serious chances. I never know if I'll become the next victim of some crazy man who needs to kill a young girl just for the fun of it.

I've been picked up by the police a few times. My pimp had provided me with phony identification because I was a minor. I never told my real name to the police except once when I felt so depressed and tired that I just couldn't go on. I don't think that I expected the police to really help me, but I still wished that there had been a way out for me.

COMMUNITY RESPONSE

The police contacted my mother, but she only told them that she was glad to be rid of me and that she wanted nothing to do with that "little slut." She had even said that they were wasting their time in trying to help me. The police found a social worker for me who placed me in a group-home for girls, but I couldn't stand living in that place. After about a week I ran away. The place was like a police state. They had curfews and rules for everything. You weren't even allowed to smoke there except in one room.

So at fourteen it was back to the streets for me, where I soon added working in peep shows, in live sex shows, and for an obscene telephone service to my list of accomplishments. Every day I let tricks abuse my body. I have to stop thinking in order to keep doing it. I have to transform myself into a mechanical doll. A wooden doll, who moans and groans and pretends to enjoy it, in order to get paid. Sometimes, I'm afraid that they'll kill me, and other times I almost hope that they would.

Author's Note

I began my research for *On the Streets: The Lives of Adolescent Prostitutes* with years of investigative reporting behind me. As a staff reporter for a New York City newspaper, I had published articles on political corruption, nursing home scandals, landlord abuse, and urban gangs. I had also written over a dozen books, many on contemporary issues. At times my stories were disturbing but needed to be told. As a journalist, I thought I had seen it all. But I was wrong. I hadn't yet discovered the world of adolescent and child prostitution.

The research for this book took me to pimp bars, peep shows, and massage parlors. I called classified ads in magazines designed to sell sex. I interviewed children selling themselves on street corners and in game arcades. My research guided me through the ugliest tour of urban America possible. The profiles in this book are composites of the young people I interviewed, written to protect their identity and yet reveal some of the sordid details of their daily lives.

As many of these young people appeared even more desperate than they were willing to admit, most of the interviews took place in various eating places. Girls who had pimps and nightly quotas to meet usually chose fast food places because they were anxious to return to the street. They knew that they needed to earn still more money before they returned home.

I was surprised at the openness of these young people. They were anxious to tell their stories and in many cases seemed to enjoy the recognition of being heard as individuals. I had the feeling that despite the topic of this text, many liked the idea of being interviewed for a book.

The most difficult part of my research was sharing time with the adolescents who were still actively engaged in prostitution. In addition to my tape recorder and notebook, I always brought along a list of resources where they could find help in their area. After a while I stopped being surprised when I discovered that they were already knowledgeable about those community services. Some had had negative experiences, some were too afraid of their pimps to go for help, others were so filled with desperation and self-hate that they were unable to do anything for themselves.

In each case I always left my home phone number in the event that they changed their minds. They were told that calling collect was acceptable. Out of eighty-seven people I talked to, only one girl called. She left a message on my answering machine, but when I returned her call she refused to speak to me. Her roommate told me that she had changed her mind.

94

AUTHOR'S NOTE

The prostitution of youth is perhaps the worst abuse that can befall a minor. Child and adolescent prostitution exists because society allows it to exist. I was often told that this crime continues because it involves only "forgotten" young people. Yet in actuality, these adolescents have the potential to be as valuable to themselves and to society as any teenager. Each is a unique and special human being. Their pain as well as their humanity makes them unforgettable. And we must remember that they are still out there—on the streets.

Bibliography

Bracey, Dorothy H. *Baby Pros: Preliminary Profiles of Juvenile Prostitutes,* New York: John Jay Press, 1979.

Carem, Arlene & Moody, Howard. *Working Women: The Subterranean World of Street Prostitution.* New York: Harper & Row, 1985.

Drew, Dennis, & Drake, Jonathan. *Boys for Sale.* Miami Beach: Brown Books, 1969.

Goldstein, Paul. *Prostitution and Drugs.* Lexington, MA: Lexington Books, 1979.

Madison, Arnold. *Runaway Teens: An American Tragedy.* New York: Lodestar Books, 1979.

Sereny, Gitta, & Wilson, Victoria. *The Invisible Children: Child Prostitution In America, West Germany, and Great Britain.* New York: Knopf, 1985.

Index

INDEX

homosexuality, 43–44, 48–52

Huckleberry House Project, 41, 45

incest, 38–39, 45–46

Interpol, 75

James, Jennifer, 47

law enforcement agencies, 78–82

love cons, 23–26

male prostitutes, 53–64
  child pornography and, 60–62
  drugs and, 57–58
  heterosexuality of, 55
  homosexuality and, 43–44, 48–52, 55
  medical treatment and, 51, 83
  in nineteenth century, 69–70
  at video game arcades, 1, 52, 54

medical services, 82–85

National Institutes of Mental Health, 41, 47, 83–84

nineteenth century prostitution, 65–75

parental relationships, 41

peep shows, 34, 91

Pelvic Inflammatory Disease, 20–21

pimps, 22–37
  demands of, 24–25
  drugs provided by, 28–29, 66–67
  ploys used by, 22–29
  prosecution of, 79–80
  relationships of prostitutes and, 22–26
  runaways and, 22–23
  seasoning tactics of, 28–31
  terrorizing by, 27–28
  at transport terminals, 22–23, 26

police programs, 80–82

pregnancy, 7–8, 82

procurement, 22–23, 26, 33, 53–54
  abduction and, 28–29, 72–74
  by prostitution rings, 58–59

prostitution rings, 28, 34, 58–60, 75–77

Robinson, Greg, 64

runaways, 1, 2, 26–28, 34, 59, 85–86

runaway shelters, 85–87, 91

sadism, 28, 32, 53

saloon girls, 65, 66–67

Sanger, William W., 67

sexual abuse, 23, 38–39, 45–46

sexually transmitted diseases, 50–52, 63, 82, 83

INDEX

About the Author

Elaine Landau received her B.A. degree from New York University in English and Journalism and a Master's degree in Library and Information Science from Pratt Institute.

She has worked as a newspaper reporter, an editor, and a librarian, but believes that many of her most fascinating as well as rewarding hours have been spent researching and writing books and articles on contemporary issues for young people.

Ms. Landau makes her home in New York City.